Be Your Own Boss!

Used Car Dealership
Business Startup

A Detail Step By Step Guide to Starting a Successful Preowned Car Lot Business for All 50 States

By

Jack Porter

Published by:

Streets of Dream
Press

Streets of Dream Press

Cover & Interior designed

By

Jackie Bretford

First Edition

Contents

Introduction

Congratulations on taking the first step to getting started with forming a used car dealership. I have been in the car retail and sales space for over 30 years.

These days, I am enjoying a relaxing retirement, doing what I have truly enjoyed most about one aspect of my career in sales - giving back.

I spent the majority of my career being a trusted therapist, minus the couch. I was the equal partner that my clients needed, and they were the lifeblood of my success.

During my time as a salesman, I was able to learn industry secrets, increase my knowledge, and gain skills that allowed me to help my customers maneuver through the world of buying a new or used car. Since retiring, I haven't been able to pass on that knowledge, until now.

Car dealerships have been an integral part of the US economy. The auto industry has been the heart of our American culture for centuries.

In addition to being a hugely rewarding career, starting a used car dealership can be a very profitable venture.

The NADA (National Automobile Dealers Association), reported at the beginning of 2017 that the median profit for car dealerships was averaging about $850,000. This figure is a combination of both new and used car sales.

As of this writing, there are an estimated over 200 million licensed automobile drivers on the road, and more than 250 million vehicles are registered in the United States.

If it appears that there are more cars on the road than people already, how could you possibly make any money in this industry?

If you are wondering how you can start a used car dealership and build a sustainable and viable business, there are a few things you need to consider about this ever-expanding industry as a whole.

For starters, it is quite common for households to have more than one car. The reality of the matter is that most people cannot find legitimate justification for investing in a new car versus a used car. The reason for that is the second you drive a new car off the dealership floor it continues to depreciate in value by a whopping 40% over the first 5 years.

This doesn't do anything to hurt the new automobile dealership, but the owner suffers when trying to resell the vehicle. This is why many people opt to purchase a slightly used vehicle that they can get at significantly below market value.

This makes used car purchases extremely popular. They comprise the majority of the industry's sales. For this reason, starting a used car dealership can prove to be extremely lucrative for those who have the dedication and financial resources to make it happen.

Despite what you may have heard or read, starting and operating a used car dealership necessitates that you possess more than just an inherent ability to sell things.

You also need to be able to follow through and hang in there through the intricate licensure process. You also must be able to cover the startup expenses and costs involved in operating a used car dealership, continue to cover expenses each month, and consistently keep an inventory on your car lot.

Make sure you complete the necessary preliminary steps before you start operating your car dealership to avoid the pitfalls of a failed business and investment.

This book is designed to help you navigate the murky waters of starting a car dealership based on my 30 plus years of industry knowledge and expertise.

This is the ultimate way that I can give back, and I truly hope you find the information here helpful.

By the time you finish reading this book, you will learn how to consider all the options before starting your business. This means doing your research and deciding on how to operate as a dealership.

Will you open one location, or will you open multiple? Do you want to create your own brand, or do you want to purchase a franchise with an existing infrastructure?

All of those questions and more are important to consider before even starting your used car dealership.

Next, we will go over the "why." Why a car dealership, and why used cars?

I alluded to the "why" here in the introduction with the value of new and used cars, but we will dive more into the nuances behind this thought process and buying behavior. In addition, we will look at the selling side of used car dealerships from the customer perspective. Then we'll examine some common industry statistics for revenue generation.

We will cover the necessities you need to get started with opening your used car dealership. These necessities include financing, picking a location, getting registered, adding inventory, and expert fees.

We will also review the dealer software available, how to pick your qualified and skilled employees, and obtaining licensing and insurance.

All of that information will then be used to complete your business plan. You will not be able to obtain financing without a well-written and concise business plan.

We will review the major sections of the business plan you need to focus on, and how to complete all of the necessary documentation for approval. We'll also discuss how to maintain your licensure and documentation once you obtain it.

After you have put your business plan together, we will move on to look at all of the details involved in operating your used car dealership.

We will examine details like how to get new inventory, how to maintain your lot, warranties you can offer to customers, and how to maintain excellent customer standards and practices.

One of the most underrated methods of obtaining inventory for your lot is auctions. In this section, we will also review the different types of auctions, auctions with the kinds of cars you want, where to find them, and how to join. I'll even show you what cars to buy and what cars to avoid buying to save you heartache down the line.

After you have purchased your inventory, we will talk about how to prepare it for sale. This means preparing the vehicle itself as well as marketing and promotional efforts to let people know you have a new car or cars on the lot.

This leads us to a more in-depth discussion on how to market and advertise properly and how to meet customer expectations and assess their needs.

I will even show you ways you can earn more profit through alternative methods of making money while you build your physical location and open your doors to the public.

Then, we get into the good stuff of how to actually turn a profit in this business. We will break down the key tips when pricing your inventory, as well as how you earn a commission on the front and back end of a sale.

From there, we look at customer satisfaction practices to keep happy customers who repeatedly return to your business. We will examine alternative financing and purchasing options for buyers of all backgrounds and personas.

You can get started operating and running your own used car dealership relatively easily with minimal out-of-pocket expenses if you ask the right questions and make the right decisions.

As a bonus, I have included a state by state guide for the specific licensure and pricing requirements for all 50 states. Find your state and review the requirements, so you know where to get started.

You can also find a mass amount of information related to starting a used car dealership online, but the problem with that is not all advice is sound.

When you start your business on false advice, then you run the huge risk of starting out on the wrong side of the street and never being able to cross back to the other side.

This book is going to give you the tools you need to get licensed and run a compliant and fully operational car dealership in your area.

Simply apply the principles and techniques you learn here, and you will be well on your way to starting a used car dealership.

Chapter 1: The Basics

Other car dealers like myself sell used cars and primarily focus on niche targeting to a specialized segment. I chose to open a brick and mortar facility selling used cars.

I've seen others create used car dealerships online while offering custom or luxury car dealerships that also exist both online and in brick and mortar locations.

For the sake of this book, we will only focus on the brick and mortar aspect of operating a used car dealership.

The Impact of the Used Car Industry

In the early 2000s, around 2005, I was in the height of my career as a car dealer. Back then there were about 40 million used cars being sold all over the country compared to the meager 17 million new cars. That figure is less than half of the total of used cars sold.

The average cost of a used vehicle is about $9,000. The auto industry has more than 130,000 registered, used car dealerships alone that employ thousands upon thousands of people.

The used car industry is growing simply because of the economy calls for us to be more fiscally conservative. Often, it is a life or death necessity to cut spending habits when it relates to what many see as a luxury - cars.

One of the many things that draw aspiring entrepreneurs to the used car dealership business model is that to start a modest shop, not selling high-end vehicles at first is extremely uncomplicated and financially realistic.

This made it quite easy for me to transition to my own car dealership. I started from the comfort of my home before I ever opened the doors or put one single car on a lot.

You too can easily open your doors without ever getting a loan from a bank. We will discuss that later on in this book.

The money seems great and is certainly a huge incentive to open and start your used car dealership. First, ask yourself why you should choose this path versus maybe opening a restaurant?

Why Start a Used Car Dealership

I believe that since you are reading this book, you are interested in the industry extensively, and may have even asked yourself why so many people who buy cars for the very first time typically buy a used car? The answer is clean and clear-cut.

Money.

The cost of purchasing a brand new car is usually financially out of the reach of the ordinary hard-working individual. This individual merely wants to own their own car hence the surging demand for used cars all across the country.

Surprisingly, this demand for used cars is widespread, especially in newly developed countries that are not known for manufacturing cars.

Used car dealerships do exactly what it sounds like they do. They sell used cars to eager buyers.

Apart from being known as dealerships that sell used cars, they are also a great resource for sellers who want to get rid of their cars but don't have the resources or knowledge to do so.

What these dealerships do is purchase used cars at a discounted price, then resell them at a price that assures a profit.

Selling used cars allows you, as the dealer, to earn a profit while experiencing the use and variety of different cars from your car lot until you have a chance to get them sold.

Sit down and brainstorm about the types of car models that people tend to favor or buy the most in your city before putting inventory on your lot.

Analyze all the available demographics of the customers who are most likely to purchase a used car. Examine qualities such as the style of car they prefer, the age of the car, and most importantly, the cost.

After you have accomplished that, be prepared to grow your used car lot into a thriving dealership.

Initial Considerations

Before you decide to host a parade down your street, open your dealership doors, and begin pairing customers to cars, there's a bit of prerequisite work that must be accomplished.

While these pre-grand opening steps might seem boring and unexciting, they could very well be the difference between your continued success or ultimate failure.

Let's review the five most important action steps you need to consider before opening your dealership.

Market Research

If there is a huge demand for used cars in your city, you are in a position to put your dealership on the path to lucrative profits. Likewise, if there isn't, it could have damaging effects on your brand before you even open.

Select your retail location for your dealership lot. Make sure to do your research on the number of used cars purchased within ten miles of that retail spot. Look at all the data over the course of a year.

For those with favorable stats, research those purchases a little further, to find out the percentage of types of cars being sold (SUVs vs. cars, for example).

Be sure to pay special attention to the car makes and models that sell more often than others.

Lastly, make records of the competition in the area, as well as what services, discounts, and incentives they currently offer.

Your goal with the research is to determine where the unfulfilled need is for the used car market in your area. Then you can set about fulfilling the need and operating with extreme confidence.

Look at the Numbers

Please do not confuse the idea of running a used car dealership with operating a successful and profitable dealership.

In order for you to get a better understanding of the potential urgency and demand for used cars in your city, you'll need to plan out some figures. You do that by determining the number of used cars purchased or sold in your city each year, then evaluate the percentage of the industry that you will be the most successful at dominating.

Finally, by finding the median profit margin per vehicle sold, you can gauge how much of a profit your particular car dealership stands to make on an annual basis if operating at 100% efficiency.

The Low-Hanging Fruit

Your potential and existing customers are the single most critical factor in the success or lack thereof in your dealership. Take the time to find out who these low-hanging fruit are, and what it is they care about the most.

This research is extremely vital. Review the types of vehicles you plan on adding to your inventory, ensuring they make sense for where you live.

Do some additional research to determine specific characteristics of your target audience like their age, gender, family status, average income, and people who own similar types of vehicles.

There is plenty of statistical data available on the internet. In the future, this will allow you to customize your marketing, advertising dollars, and efforts towards those customers who are most likely to be in need or interested in what your dealership has to offer.

Be sure to form any of your inferences regarding your target audience from factual, actionable information. Don't merely make unfounded assumptions. That is a huge mistake and one that can be costly in the end.

To Franchise or Not to Franchise Part 1

Starting and running a used car dealership from the ground up is a highly rewarding but potentially risky career choice. Because of this, some dealership owners opt to go the franchise route instead.

When you franchise, people with little to no capital or credit can enter into a franchise agreement with a bigger, more financially secure car manufacturer.

This means that the car manufacturer allows the franchisee the right to use established branding and marketing materials and to participate in promotional deals.

The car manufacturer also helps to supply the dealership with quality used automobiles. In return, the dealership owner is required to prove that he or she has the money and the talent to be able to operate the dealership and turn an acceptable profit.

The car manufacturer will likely also take a significant portion of those profits both as an initial fee and as an annual due.

Given that the dealership will be able to benefit from associating with an established manufacturer, the overall rewards are often more than enough to offset the costs.

We will discuss the benefits and pitfalls of whether or not to be a franchise in a later chapter detailing the day-to-day running of a dealership.

Service

When dealing with used cars, you will find that when compared to newer models, they are more likely to have more of a need for upkeep than new models straight off of the factory floor.

When you include a service department in your dealership model, you'll be better suited to provide your customers with repairs, testing of emissions from their car, and various other maintenance-related services.

In addition, you'll be better equipped to estimate and appraise the cars brought in through sales or trade.

Service departments are one of the most effective ways to convey confidence to your potential used-car buyers. These buyers then will have peace of mind knowing that, should something go awry with their warranty-covered car you'll be able to fix the issues effortlessly.

Similarly, highly-ranked service departments have the potential to bring in new customers. These customers may be so impressed with the quality of service being performed that they elect to buy their used car from your dealership versus from your competition.

Start-Up Costs and Financing Options

What expenses do I need to have taken care of right away so I can be operational as quickly as possible?

While you are going to need a retail location, a lawyer's consultation, and a CPA to help you with your finances and business financial planning, you won't need those to start operating your used car dealership at the very beginning stages.

Start-Up Costs

What	Cost
LLC Registration	$50-630 Depending on your state. See the list of States in the appendix.

Inventory	$0 Floor Plan Credit. We will discuss this in the next section.
Equipment	$50 - $200 Phone, Computer, Fax, Internet, Office Equipment, etc.
Auto Dealer License	$100 - $200 Depending on your state. See the list in the appendix.
Auto Dealer Bond	$250 - $1,500 for a Minimum $25,000 bond.
Liability Insurance	General liability for your dealership can run from 20-40%, as a down payment on the yearly premium.

Starting your used car dealership is an extremely lucrative and rewarding challenge. You do not need much to start out, and as I mentioned, you can even do so from the comfort of your home office with minimal energy or capital needed.

When the time comes for you to get your retail location and more inventory, there are ways you can explore external sources of funding early in the process. Have a viable plan in place, just waiting for the trigger to be pulled.

Fortunately, there are many options when it comes to financing your auto dealership dreams.

So that you will have an idea of where to start your research, let's review the easiest and most commonly preferred financing methods outside of traditional bank loans.

Financing Your Used Car Dealership

Floor Plan Credit

The term "floor plan credit" or "floor plan financing" is quite common in the auto dealer industry and especially among those that are deep into the auction scene.

This term means a credit line exclusively given for vehicle inventory purchases. This differs from a credit card type of credit.

The difference is that credit cards are typically issued by a bank to a person or a company who can then turn around and buy personal items with the money the bank has loaned them.

The credit card holder pays interest on the borrowed funds. The credit card holder can make partial payments to pay off their balance, or they can pay it off in full.

With floor plan financing, a bank or funding agency issues a line of credit to an auto dealer. The dealer uses their floor plan credit to buy the inventory they need from auctions and other sources of vehicle stock.

There is a "sell by date" in the contract that lists the date that a car must be sold before a fee is charged.

As the dealer sells off their inventory a piece at a time, they then pay off the balance of the floor plan credit plus interest. The main goal of floor plan financing is to free up the available cash on hand a dealer has access to.

This allows you, as a used car dealership, to make amazing profits and still have funds available to work for the business.

The types of companies that issue floor plan financing or credit are highly and expertly acclimated to the car dealer industry.

Some of them also offer title services, records, and document management services.

Although floor financing can seem to be a bit confusing, it is an extremely useful strategy for car dealers who don't have a lot of capital or cash to purchase inventory.

If you live in the southern states of Georgia, South Carolina, North Carolina, or Tennessee, check out Dealers Finance. This site is a great resource for floor financing for your used car dealership in the southeast US.

Retail/Real Estate Specific Location Financing

Aside from inventory, the biggest cost of operating a used car dealership is obtaining a retail location.

Not everyone has a trust fund or excellent credit to help them get a $20,000 a month retail space, nor does anyone really like the idea of spending that much each month.

That's why I chose to buy my own showroom and office locations after years of saving whatever cash I could. This is certainly not the cheapest route, but it is an option if you have the capital available.

Financing the purchase of your retail space allows you to avoid the high monthly rent, and there are numerous financing options available. These options are based on zoning districts, location, and more factors. There are plenty of third-party lenders willing to invest for a percentage of the return.

You can find more about small business commercial real-estate loans at FitSmallBusiness.com (https://fitsmallbusiness.com/commercial-real-estate-loans/).

Small Business Administration (SBA)

If you are unable to go the traditional route of bank loans, the US government's Small Business Administration (SBA) program has many loan programs from lenders across the country for you to choose from. "Even those with bad credit may qualify for startup funding." https://www.sba.gov/funding-programs/loans

There are certain eligibility requirements that your business must meet to acquire an SBA loan.

- The business must be for-profit, officially registered, and operating legally.
- The business must be physically located and operate in the US.
- The business owner must have invested equity in the business.
- All other financing options must have been exhausted already.

Check the SBA site weekly to ensure you are not missing out on specific auto dealer programs and opportunities.

You can even talk to an advisor about their traditional loan programs for small businesses and minority-owned businesses if you are eligible.

Peer-to-Peer Financing

Obtaining adequate financing for your used car dealership does not have to be a major challenge, despite what you may be reading online.

Online and traditional methods of financing may not be an option for everyone who faces bad credit issues or who have no capital for collateral.

This doesn't mean this is the end of the line for your dream.

In these cases, more and more starter used car dealerships are relying on peer-to-peer lending.

The loan amounts are typically much smaller – $25,000 or below. There are websites out there like Prosper.com (https://www.prosper.com/) that allow you to post a tailored listing with your loan requirements.

Potential investors will be able to review your complete profile and request to determine whether or not you are suited for their financing.

Please keep in mind that while peer-to-peer lending is an absolutely great workaround to traditional methods, it should not be the end-all solution for your dealership's monetary needs. Instead, it can be an excellent temporary solution for more difficult challenges or for time constraints.

Remember to do your research. Review the basics of what you need to get started. You can start your own car dealership from your home office as early as next week!

Chapter 2: What You Need to Start

Stay compliant.

In order to legally run a car dealership in the US, you are going to need to obtain a license to sell cars of any kind.

The restrictions and processes that go along with acquiring your dealership license will vary depending on which state you live. This is why DMV.org (https://www.dmv.org/) has established a useful resource itemizing the requirements for licensure by state.

If you have plans to do any construction work or remodeling any structures on your lot, you'll also need to obtain building permits issued by your local government.

You will also need to have adequate insurance to protect your business against a myriad of scenarios.

In addition to a basic property insurance policy, you will also need to obtain liability insurance with a $75,000 surety bond.

These types of coverage are required in order to help defend not only you and your dealership but also your potential buyers and customers.

Therefore, it is a necessary aspect of buying and selling used cars as an authorized dealer.

Let's look at the other legal requirements, processes, and the paperwork needed to get started.

Legal Requirements and Licensure

Legal Requirements

It is no secret that used and new car dealerships endure multiple challenges in keeping up with the ever-increasing and strict auto dealership rules, laws, and regulations ordained by the federal and state government.

Please do not get overwhelmed and elect to skip on the regulatory aspects of your used car operation.

You could suffer from crippling fines and penalties down the line that could force you out of business.

Find a company that you can work with who specializes in assisting auto dealer owners with implementing the proper conformity. These companies can assist with these procedures and ultimately protect dealerships from those fines and possible criminal charges for not following the law.

To make sure you are staying within compliance, let's review the 10 most critical laws and regulations for the automotive industry. You should be fully aware of these laws, if not at least familiar with their names. Of course, do more research as these regulations update periodically.

Gramm-Leach-Bliley Act Privacy Rule (GLBA). The GLBA Privacy Rule is one that requires all auto dealerships to protect and safeguard their customer's information and privacy as it relates to personal and sensitive information.

This particular act regulates how auto dealerships are able to gather, store, and share a customer's personal and financial data.

Auto dealers are required to take the necessary steps and measures to disseminate to each of their customers exactly how their information is stored, shared, and collected.

Gramm-Leach-Bliley Act Safeguards Rule. In addition to the privacy rule, the GLBA also regulates that auto dealers take actual steps in the securing of information.

This means they must have a written security and information plan in place with a detailed and outlined analysis of risk, along with other factors.

Financial budgets must include funds specifically earmarked for the compliance or risk assessment of information security in any car dealership.

Failure to do so could result in fines and penalties.

Disposal Rule. The "disposal rule" is a federal mandate that requires all car dealerships who partake in the collection of consumer credit reports to safely dispose of them in such a way that protects their customer's privacy.

You can review the FTC proper disposal guidelines (https://www.ftc.gov/tips-advice/business-center/guidance/disposing-consumer-report-information-rule-tells-how) here. They include guidelines as to proper paper shredding and digital record removal.

It is up to you as the auto dealership owner to ensure consumer reports aren't laying around on your sales team's desks and unaccounted for.

Used Car Rule. This regulation mandates that auto dealers post a buyer's guide before offering a used vehicle for sale.

This guide must include information on the car's warranty, an advisory to have the car inspected by a mechanic before the purchase, and information about the major mechanical and electrical systems in the car.

Dealers must be sure that this guide is posted "prominently and conspicuously" on any used car for sale.

Equal Credit Opportunity Act. Because you are considered to be a lender of sorts as a car dealer, you must comply with all ECOA rules and laws.

That means you cannot discriminate who you sell cars to on the basis of anything like gender, race, religion, nationality, sexual orientation, or age.

These factors can also not come into consideration when considering financing for the vehicle as well. The law makes it clear that dealers must notify each applicant on the status of their application and any report taken, as well as any information used in making that decision.

Red Flags Rule. These are laws that require all auto dealerships to have a written rule in place that detects and protects your customers against common identity theft scams.

This procedure includes checking for alarming and suspicious documentation and unusual changes in customer credit history.

Auto dealers must be sure they are proactive in how they are protecting their customer's against identity theft and also following the "Red Flags Rule."

You can review the Identity Theft Protection Plan (ITPP) here (https://www.ftc.gov/tips-advice/business-center/guidance/fighting-identity-theft-red-flags-rule-how-guide-business).

IRS Form 8300. As an auto dealership, you might come into contact with large amounts of cash by selling used cars.

As a result, it is required that all cash payments received in the amount of $10,000 or more, must be filed on IRS Form 8300 (https://www.irs.gov/businesses/small-businesses-self-employed/form-8300-and-reporting-cash-payments-of-over-10000). This form is used by the IRS and Financial Crimes Enforcement Network (FinCEN) to protect against money laundering.

The IRS even includes a list of frequently asked questions and scenarios specifically aimed at auto dealerships in regards to Form 8300. You can download Form 8300 for FREE at this link: https://www.irs.gov/pub/irs-pdf/f8300.pdf.

Office of Foreign Assets Control (OFAC). The OFAC oversees and administers the economic and trade penalties, also known as sanctions, against specific countries and groups of people.

These sanctions are specifically against those who are suspected or proven to have connections to terrorism, drug trafficking, and other high crimes.

Auto dealers are by law required to verify customers' names against the "Specially Designated Nationals List" at https://sanctionssearch.ofac.treas.gov/.This is a list of people and groups monitored and targeted by OFAC.

OSHA 29 CFR 1910.157. Almost every business is required to have an emergency action plan to "facilitate and organize employer and employee actions during workplace emergencies." This ordinance also applies to auto dealerships.

Your company must have this written document prepared to protect employees and comply with OSHA standards.

Regulation Z. Regulation Z is also referred to as the "Truth in Lending Act."

You may hear some call it the "lemon laws."

This particular law requires that anyone who does financial lending, including used car dealers, openly disclose any and all of the credit terms in a way that customers can easily understand.

That also involves using standard language and explanation of rates and fees in the written terms of any loan documents and financial disclosures.

Once you understand the laws, let's examine what further licenses and paperwork you'll be required to fulfill.

Licensure and Paperwork

Every state in the country mandates specific requirements for obtaining a vehicle dealership license.

As a former car dealership owner, I understand how difficult and daunting the entire process can seem.

To help make it a bit easier, I've gathered detailed easy-to-follow dealership license instructions for each state and included them as an appendix at the end of this book. The same information can be obtained on the DMV website in your state.

You won't find rambling paragraphs overloaded with confusing legal jargon. The DMV has made the information as easy to understand as possible with bare-minimum facts.

The majority of the DMV state sites present consumers with information in bulleted lists. This concise list makes getting your dealership licensing as easy as reading your grandmother's recipe for apple pie.

All of the information gathered in the appendix from the DMV is state specific. Not only will you be advised of which applications you need to complete and submit, but you will also be informed if any of the documents require a notarized seal or must be accompanied by a fee.

Creating a Business Plan

First and most importantly, prior to taking any action, regardless of the type or size of business you plan on starting, it is most wise to plan and write out a solid and realistic business plan.

This is one of the things you can craft from your home office while you apply for your business license and insurance.

I strongly recommend that you not skip on creating a business plan. To successfully run and operate a used car dealership requires you have a great business plan in place.

Consider your business plan as the guiding blueprint that is required in order to run your auto dealership successfully.

With a practical business plan for your auto dealership, you will lessen the trial and error phase of doing business. You will be more equipped to command your business and employees with intent and caution. You will be able to understand and see in writing what to do at each phase of your business and be better equipped to handle objections and growth.

Make sure your business plan can pass the "reality test." Focus only on using facts and figures and other direct evidence from the industry as it relates to the location you plan on opening your used car dealership lot.

As you write your business plan, keep in mind the goal is not to just have a document full of facts and figures that sits on the shelf to collect dust.

It's also not wise to create one just to say you have one in place and never use the information and research contained within.

The whole idea of writing a business plan is not just for the sake of having a business document, but it is a detailed guide on how to effectively run your business from scratch.

Your business plan needs to detail and outline strategies for how you aim to oversee your used car dealership. The general rule of thumb when writing a business plan is to remain as much as possible within realistic guidelines and not ever over-calculate when adding in figures for sales volume, profits, and losses.

To be completely honest, it is wiser to undervalue items when creating a business plan, so you won't be let down when the reality is not what you had in your business plan.

Let's look at a few of the key sections of the business plan where you need to spend the majority of your energy.

The Executive Summary

This section is all about the conceptualization of your auto dealership, descriptions of your business, your business' vision declaration or statement, your dealership mission statement, and where your dealership lot will eventually be located.

In this section, you will also indicate if you plan on importing or exporting used cars to and from foreign countries or opening dealerships in other cities in the USA.

As with any other business model, including when starting a used car dealership lot, several factors influence the cost that is going to be required to successfully launch the lot with a full inventory.

These factors that influence your starting costs include:

- The location you intend on opening your dealership
- The type of used vehicles you want to sell
- The size of the dealership lot you want to start
- The current state of the economy

Every one of these factors will have a major influence on when and where you plan on starting your auto dealership business.

Other Sections

Some of the key sections of the business plan include.

- The consignment or resale business plan product offering
- SWOT analysis
- Competitive analysis
- Marketing and sales analysis and strategies
- Target market
- Market goals
- Pricing
- Costing and financial projection
- Publicity and advertising strategy
- Expansion and growth strategies
- Budget and startup capital.

Advice for a Sound Business Plan

Write to captivate your investors.

Start today. You can always adjust the plan later. Your plan is wrong the day you print it!

The business plan life cycle is on-going. First, you write the plan. Then you run the plan. You are always reviewing and revising the plan. Finally, you repeat the process again.

What is a SWOT analysis?

SWOT stands for Strength, Weakness, Opportunities, and Threats. Think of a SWOT analysis as the detailed pros and cons list of opening your business.

Strengths are internal positive factors.

Weaknesses are the internal negative ones.

Opportunities are external positive factors.

Threats are the external negative ones.

This diagram will help you in determining your SWOT analysis.

Strengths (internal, positive factors)	Weaknesses (internal, negative factors)
Strengths describe the positive attributes, tangible and intangible, of your organization. These are within your control.	Weaknesses are aspects of your business that detract from the value you offer or place you at a competitive disadvantage.
Opportunities (external, positive factors)	Threats (external, negative factors)
Opportunities are external attractive factors that represent reasons for your business to exist and prosper.	Threats are external factors beyond your control that could put your business at risk. You may benefit from having contingency plans for them.

Please do your research on business plan templates and guides to give you a sound starting point for an effective business plan.

Remember, use real facts and figures and data.

Equipment, Tools, and Dealer Software

Equipment and Tools

Today's world is an increasingly digital one.

That means that in order for a used car dealership to survive the fierce competition, you will need for it to be able to stay relevant in the digital world.

This means investing in the right dealer management system (DMS).

A DMS is a true necessity. We will discuss it further in the next section.

To give some context for what it is, DMS is a comprehensive software package that is explicitly executed for and implemented at dealerships.

This software assists them with the day-to-day operation, running, and record keeping of car sales, vehicle inventory, business finances, customer warranty claims, overall administration, and anything else a car dealer may require.

A superior DMS will be able to help automate sales tracking, parts ordering for the service department, and more.

Automated car dealership systems can also make great use of advanced customer relationship management (CRM) technology integrations, aiding with customer and vendor follow-up. This also provides the staff with a convenient, effective, integrated database from which they can extract significant customer-specific data.

There are tons of dealership CRM and DMS solutions available in the marketplace. Be certain to do plenty of research to find the car dealership system that exceeds your current needs while remaining affordable. Ask for a demo when available.

In addition, make investing in the proper security tools a top priority. For criminals searching for a big payoff, auto dealerships are a strangely attractive victim.

Costly merchandise, matched with the fact that many car dealers operate outdoors, means investing in the right security for your auto dealership is critical to deterring thieves from stealing your inventory.

From personal experience, digital solutions are much more effective than the security procedures of previous times passed.

Look for companies that offer remote video monitoring and 24/7 software-reinforced surveillance. This surveillance should be proficient in the recognition and evaluation of common threats, tripping silent on-site alarms, and possibly reaching out to the local authorities.

When also paired with common motion sensors and electrified gates, the perfect surveillance system can guarantee that your investment remains safe.

Dealer Software

Dealer software is one of the most important tools that you will need in your used car dealership.

The main goal of auto dealer software is to help you increase your car sales.

The industry is increasingly embracing new technology in order to get away from traditional pen and paper.

Auto dealer software enables car dealerships to automate and systematize all of their important processes.

With the ability to integrate with a majority of the CRM (Customer Relationship Management) solutions available, auto dealer software allows you to also have more control of your sales processes and customers as well as your inventory.

There are several features to look for in particular software. These features include:

- Regulatory compliance
- Credit reporting by synchronizing with credit bureaus
- VIN database records
- Repair order tracking
- Warranty and service databases

Here are my recommendations for some of the most favorable easy-to-use and implement auto dealer software available.

Marketing360 (https://www.marketing360.com/) is an auto dealership software that can assist dealerships with increasing their customer base and reach while also adding more inventory to their lot in volume.

This particular type of management software automates mundane and repetitive marketing functions. It can create and oversee marketing campaigns for selling your used vehicles via social media, managed through an interactive dashboard with reporting and analytics.

A fantastic and robust auto dealer customer relationship management (CRM) software is ELEAD1ONE (https://www.elead-crm.com/).

This software is a great tool for helping you maintain communication with your customers through multiple channels. You can call, text, email them, and even interact with them on social media sites. This serves as a help center or repair command hub.

This particular type of auto dealer software can assist your sales team in managing their book of business with streamlined communications.

Bit Dealer Software (https://www.bitdms.com/) is an auto dealer solution for you to manage your important customer orders, lot inventory, sales stats, and various other data on the front and back end. Typically this information would require a manual data entry.

This software will enable you to enter and store important customer files and information simply through their license or ID number.

The software is also capable of sending automated reminders via text messaging to your current client list about when their vehicle needs to be serviced.

This is by no means a comprehensive list. Find software that is going to provide the features you need to help make running your auto dealership easier.

Look at the challenges you may be facing then find an auto dealer software that can help you solve those challenges.

Let's look at some examples of challenges that used car dealerships face. This can help you examine the proper solution.

Common Challenges Dealers Face

Managing Multiple Locations

A common issue that used car dealerships with many locations or franchises face is streamlining communication and information among multiple locations.

A cloud-based auto dealer software will allow you to centralize all of the important data that needs to be shared among the locations. This way, everyone can collaborate effectively with each other, other car dealerships, and vendors.

Managing Inventory and Car Parts

As you acquire your inventory, you will need to have a place to keep all of the information about the car in one place, and easily place it on your website.

With this type of software, you can also automate the reordering of parts when you get low, or you can simply set it up to notify your service department to do so.

Maintaining Customer Information and Documents

Auto dealership software will allow you to create your own applications and forms, personalize business documents based on customer credit and loan amounts, and also streamline additional services like obtaining insurance. It even allows you to quickly and easily run credit reports with a linked account to all of the three major credit bureaus.

Next, we'll examine how to get your hands on the cars you want to sell.

Chapter 3: How to Obtain Quality Inventory

There are a few ways to obtain the inventory for your used car lot.

You can get a car through a customer trade-in, you can outright purchase cars from the public such as in a "we buy cars" campaign, or you can buy cars from an auction.

We will discuss your auction house options in-depth in this section, as most of your inventory will likely be from this source.

Reputable auction houses are members of the National Auto Auction Association (NAAA). The members of this organization are held to higher standards such as operating in secure, neutral auction settings.

You can find a listing of auctions that are part of the NAAA at https://www.naaa.com/.

Copart Auto Auctions

"Copart is a global leader in online car auctions and a premier destination for the resale and remarketing of vehicles. Specializing in salvage vehicle auctions, Copart makes it easy for Members to find, bid on, and win the vehicles that they are looking for. From salvage cars to clean title vehicles, Members can bid on classics, early and late model cars and trucks, motorcycles, industrial vehicles and more." (https://www.copart.com/)

Salvage auctions for cars offer used car dealers with an opportunity to get an even better deal. There are things to keep in mind when going to the salvage auctions.

Unlike visiting regular auction houses or online auctions, salvage vehicles require a little bit more of a time commitment to get the car ready for purchase off your lot.

When you attend a salvage auction, you are specifically purchasing a vehicle or vehicles that have previously been in an accident or damaged so badly that the owner's insurance company refuses to insure it any longer and writes it off as a complete loss.

The insurance company will then take claim of the vehicle and sell it to one of these salvage auctions on consignment in the hopes of recovering at least a small portion of their loss.

There are a few key things you want to keep in mind when getting your inventory at the salvage auctions. Most importantly, always remember that these vehicles by law are deemed not drivable in their existing condition.

No matter what it looks like on the outside, be very mindful that you are going to need to complete some repairs in order to get the vehicle back on the road safely for the buyer. A common term for this is "street-legal" among dealers.

Each state has its own set of rules, laws, and regulations regarding the purchasing, disposal, designation and reselling of salvaged vehicles. Check with your state department to determine what percentage of damage constitutes a salvaged car.

In Indiana, for example, it may cost you 50% of the vehicle's total value to repair it. Whereas in Ohio, it may costs you closer to 80%.

Because these vehicles are not drivable by law, you are going to need to arrange to have them towed from the auction site. Most of the bigger salvage auctions, like Copart, offer delivery of your purchase for an additional cost.

Check with the particular auction site beforehand to determine what that is so you can be sure you have enough for the purchase price plus delivery.

Doing your research and due diligence when it comes to auctions and salvage auctions, in particular, is a critical part of your business. It does not, however, have to be difficult.

If you are willing to dive in with your sleeves rolled up, and get your hands dirty, then you can come across many great deals.

Copart is the biggest salvage auction in the country. There are others that can easily be found in your local area by doing a Google search.

My top three favorites in the online marketplace are Automix, Capital Auto Auctions, Salvage Auto, and Copart.

Let's talk about how to get a membership and bid on these cars; then we'll talk about what not to buy at the salvage yards to avoid making costly mistakes.

How to Become a Member

Before you can start bidding or buying on the cars available on the Copart auction site, as with any other auction site, you need to get registered and pay your membership fee. There are several membership levels that come with different perks.

These perks include how many vehicles you can bid on, how many auctions you can join, and even the cost associated with the bidding process. There are free and paid accounts available, but know that a free account is quite limited on what it can see and do on the site.

The paid membership on Copart is $200 a year, which allows you to have unlimited access to auctions, searches, bids, and watch lists.

If you do not have your business license before joining, you will need to find a broker to represent you. My advice is to register after getting your business license.

Next, you will need to increase your buying power. If you are on a paid account, you can skip this step.

Increasing your buying power means adding a deposit of 10%, which is fully refundable if you do not win an auction. For example, if you place your bid maximum at $4,000, a deposit of $400 will need to be put down before you can even begin to bid.

Let's take a look at how you go about bidding and buying vehicles after you register.

How to Bid and Buy

Once you have registered for either a free or paid account and submitted your license, you can then begin to search any of the 100,000 plus vehicles. Keep in mind that you have a set number of searches on a free account.

You have the option of entering in all of your chosen search criteria into the search feature on the Copart site.

If you have a VIN number, you can even enter that to pull up specifics on a certain vehicle and find out when the auction is taking place for it.

You can view auctions without being logged in to your account, but you won't be able to place a valid bid on any vehicles until you register and or login.

Any vehicles over $1,000 will require you to upgrade your account or place a deposit of 10% before you start bidding. Once you are on the site, you can click on the auctions tab to view a listing of all the auctions available for the day, or you can view the calendar and plan ahead for future auctions.

With a premium account, you can attend an unlimited amount of auctions at once. Basic members can only join one at a time.

You can join an auction from a desktop or a mobile device. Auction times at Copart are always at 10am for the facilities on the east coast and 12pm for all other auction facilities.

There are also auctions in the evening that run Monday through Thursday starting at 9 pm EST. These are auctions for the leftover vehicles that didn't get sold during the day's auction.

There are two ways you can purchase a vehicle through bids. You can submit your bid prior to the auction with a maximum bid amount, or you can join the auction live. Prior to bidding, you will need to have a valid driver's license or government issued ID on file.

The preliminary bidding, which is done prior to the live auction, can take place up to one hour prior to the start. The preliminary bid is placed with increments built in. As the bids get higher, your bid increments will be presented to keep you in the running during the live auction.

If no other bid outbids your maximum, then you have won the vehicle without ever having to be present. When a tie happens between a pre-bid and the live bid, the live bidder will always win out as the highest bidder in the end.

The broker is the one to manage the pre-bid process for members and during the live auction. Copart uses its own patented vehicle auction software so that you can take part in the auction from anywhere in the world.

There is an option to bypass bidding all together with a "Buy It Now" feature, similar to the eBay auction site. This button allows you to purchase a vehicle immediately, with the funds you know you have available.

You have up to 3 working days to pay the invoice you receive for the vehicle, or it goes back on the site for relisting. You will be charged a $50 late fee for each car that is not paid within the 3-day time frame.

Once you have made the payment, then transportation is arranged either through your own methods with the salvage auction site.

There is a complimentary storage time after the auction before you will start being charged for them holding the vehicle. Know how many vehicles you plan on purchasing at each auction. Have your transportation ready and on standby or immediately arrange the third-party towing with the salvage auction site.

You are not permitted to drive these vehicles on the road as they are deemed damaged and not street legal.

Let's talk about how you get the salvaged vehicles fixed once you have them in your possession.

How to Fix the Vehicles

The repairing of salvaged vehicles is typically the most time-consuming part of the process, but it is the most gratifying.

Before you even purchase a salvaged vehicle, check with your state to determine the laws.

A salvaged vehicle's title will never have the original title designation but will be re-categorized as "rebuilt salvage." In some states, it can also be called "reconditioned."

Hire a licensed and qualified mechanic to make the repairs if you don't know how to do them yourself. Keep all of your documents and paperwork on the vehicle in a safe and secure location. Take progress photos of the vehicle before, during, and after repairs.

Once the vehicle is finished, you will need to have it inspected by the DMV. You will need to take all of your paperwork and the photos you took with you when you go as well as your proof of purchase.

The DMV typically checks for stolen parts and not necessarily if the car is legally suited for the road.

When the inspection has been passed, you will need to pay a fee and complete an application for a re-branded vehicle title.

There are vehicles that you want to stay away from when dealing with salvage auctions. Let's review what to avoid, and then look at other ways to increase your inventory through other non-salvage type auction houses.

What Not to Buy

There are 2 types of vehicles you will want to avoid at all costs - flooded and junk titled vehicles.

Always avoid flooded vehicles at salvage auctions. The reason for this is that flooded vehicles typically have ruined and water damaged electrical parts.

It may appear as though everything in the vehicle seems to be in working condition now and even after repairs. The truth is that it might not be operational a few months or years down the line.

Water corrosion is infamous for causing all types of electrical breakdowns and failures. It's hard to do enough research to find out exactly where all the water damage occurred in the vehicle.

Instead, it's best just to avoid them from the start.

Secondly, avoid junk title vehicles. In some places in the country, salvaged vehicles can be issued a "junk title" or "parts only title" for the vehicles which have been involved in major car wrecks.

These vehicles are extensively damaged and should only be transported to the nearest junkyard.

The majority of states won't even issue a new title for these vehicles, so purchasing one and fixing it up to resell is a wasted effort.

You won't be able to get a valid title for it or resell it. While some of these cars eventually do make it back on the streets, it's best to avoid them as well.

Cars can end up with a "salvage title" for just minor damage on the trunk or rear bumper all the way to extreme cases where half the front end of the car is missing.

Plenty of people may try to talk you out of going to the salvage auctions in general. The truth of the matter is that salvage title vehicles can be a huge value.

Know what to look for, avoid what not to purchase, and do not pay more than 70% of the market value of the vehicle if it has already been previously repaired.

There are regular auction houses like Manheim and ADESA that auction used and new vehicles for sale without any damage.

Let's look at how to join Manheim and how you go about bidding and buying vehicles through this approach. Many of the major auction houses are similarly operated.

Manheim Auction House

Manheim is the country's largest auction provider and vehicle remarketer. They are the premier connector of car buyers and sellers in North America. With Manheim Auctions, buyers and sellers have access to the biggest wholesale database of new and used vehicles from over 120 different auctions sites in their network.

You can find Manheim Auctions at this website https://www.manheim.com/.

Sites like Manheim are geared more towards business professionals like auto dealerships, rather than individual buyers.

The reason for this is that the company has a huge investment in technology and human capital. This ensures that auto dealers and entrepreneurs have the inventory they need and ground-breaking front-to-back solutions for inventory management and acquisition. Their specialty is in volume buyers with experienced and knowledgeable sellers.

Registration and Membership Requirements

Manheim auction site registration is currently open to auto dealers only. You can register for an event, or you can create an account on the website to give you access to the auctions.

How to Bid & Buy

Manheim gives you the ability to use Simulcast, which is their online platform. It allows dealers to participate in the auctions streamed live from anywhere in the world.

The user interface works just like any other auction's site, and each buyer has their own lane. You can also review the history of the vehicles you would like to purchase.

You can bid on more than one vehicle at a time with simultaneous auctions all over the country.

More Online Resources

There are even appraisal resources available online to help you determine if the price of the vehicle is below or above market value.

DealerCue provides dealerships with real-time, intelligent, market-driven vehicle appraisal, pricing, inventory management, and sourcing solutions.

In the following chapter, we will dive headlong into what it takes actually to operate a used car dealership in the day-to-day.

Chapter 4: Operating a Used Car Dealership

There's a big difference between simply operating a used car dealership and operating a profitable used car dealership.

To get a better idea of the possible demand for used cars in your area, you'll need to crunch some numbers. By identifying the number of used cars sold in your area every year, you can estimate what percentage of the market you'll be likely to be able to corner.

By locating the average profit per vehicle, you can get an approximate idea of how much profit your dealership stands to make per year.

While the groundwork associated with opening a dealership can be time-consuming, expensive, and demanding, the real test of your dealership's viability doesn't begin until after you open your doors to the public.

Without the right management of your dealership, all the effort you put towards laying the foundation will be wasted.

While each state has its own rules and regulations, there are several important universal aspects of operating a car dealership and tips on how you can get the most out of your investment.

Your customers are the single most important factor in the success or failure of your business, so taking the time to identify who they are and what they care about is absolutely vital.

Take a look at the types of cars you plan on selling, then do some research to determine the age, gender, and income level of the average individual who owns those types of vehicles. Later down the line, this will allow you to tailor your marketing and advertising efforts towards those who are most likely to be interested in what you have to offer.

Make sure to base any of your conclusions regarding your target clients on real actionable data; don't simply make assumptions.

Unless there's a demand for used cars in your area, your used car dealership isn't likely to turn much of a profit.

Before you really get down to business, you need to assess existing demand. Choose a potential location for your dealership, then research the number of used cars sold within ten miles of that location over the space of a year.

Research those purchases further to determine the percentage of types of vehicles being sold. Make special notes of makes and models that sell more frequently.

Finally, make a note of any competing dealerships as well as what those dealerships offer. If you can see that there is an unfulfilled demand for used cars in your area, then you should be able to move forward with confidence.

Finding the Proper Location

When opening a used car dealership, it is extremely important to focus on the exact location where you plan on pitching your business tent.

Keep in mind that a used car dealership business will be more likely to fail in higher income regions of our society. Conversely, it may be quite primed to exceed expectations and achieve success in urban or low to middle-class neighborhoods around your city.

For this reason, it is imperative that you ensure a location for your used car dealership where the middle class and the lower class of your area reside.

The reason for this location is because, in addition to getting tons of new clients that will patronize you at this location, you will also get your building and lot at a much cheaper rate versus what you would pay to open your dealership in high-class area of your community.

There many different sized used car lots all over the United States, but please keep in mind that does not mean that your dealership can thrive and survive in just any location.

You must do your research by completing a thorough feasibility study. If you have the resources to do so, perform a market survey asking people in the area their opinions and to provide feedback.

There is also quite a large possibility that you could encounter a used car dealership that has recently gone out of business in the area where you want to open your dealership.

The more you research, the more opportunities you have to find exactly what you are looking for.

When doing your market research and studies, please keep these tips in mind as a general rule of thumb.

- The population density and analysis of the location

- The buying power of the population near the location

- How easily accessible to the public the location will be

- How many used car dealerships are already in the area

- The local laws governed by your state of residence

- Analyzation of the traffic in the area, construction, and parking for your customers

While these are very important, they are not all-encompassing of what you should be considering when looking for a location.

Once you have found the perfect spot for your dealership, it's time to look for help running it.

You are going to need to hire quality employees and sales agents in order to sell vehicles, especially if you have no former sales experience selling vehicles.

In the beginning, it is completely ok to do things from home, but as the next progressive step in your business launch, you will want to consider hiring a team of staff members.

Hiring Employees and Staff

This car dealership is your baby.

It's your vision, passion, and follow-through that will see it to fruition and long-term sustainability.

Eventually, it is going to be hard for you to do everything on the back end and the front end alone. Your customers will deal mainly with whomever you have sourced and hired to fulfill your sales role.

As a former used car dealership owner, I want to caution you to avoid archaic stereotypes of what a used car salesman should be.

Nobody wants a cut-throat, high-pressure, deceptive salesperson trying to make a commission. This archetype doesn't help your business, and it certainly doesn't sell cars.

You don't want to have a reputation in the community for using shady sales tactics to sell cars.

While it may bring in a fast buck for your business, it does nothing for the public's perception of your dealership and its reputation in the long run.

People talk. Word of mouth is king!

Nobody overcomes negative public opinion once the freight train gets away from them.

Don't trick your customers into buying cars. That's not a win/win.

It's also not a win/win to get them to spend more than what the car is actually worth.

Treat your customers as an extension of your business. Think of them as a community partner, if you will, a partner who will become a brand advocate for your dealership.

You provide exceptional customer service and products, and they will reciprocally tell all their friends and family who will hopefully also choose you for those same used car needs.

Focus on sales agents who have a proven track record of putting the needs of the customer above their percentage.

Sales agents need to be disciplined, trustworthy, and supportive individuals who also recognize that a business thrives on repeat customers and sales.

One thing that I struggled with in the beginning was a high rate of staff turnover - until I got it right.

Instead of investing a lot of time and money training just anyone who wanted to work for me, I focused on finding sales agents and employees who exhibited traits of going above and beyond.

How do you do that considering so many people can fabricate their experience in order to woo you during an interview?

Advice for Interviewing Potential Candidates

Here's how I managed to weed out the ones who were merely good on paper:

1. Take good notes on how the candidate presents themselves during the interview and even in the waiting room while waiting to be interviewed. Are they nervous? Do they seem confident and self-assured?

2. How do they interact with other candidates waiting to be interviewed? This means scheduling a few people at the same time, so they are in the waiting area together. Do they interact with each other? Are they territorial and guarded? Are they social and understand the etiquette of being social in a formal context?

3. What are their qualifications and sales record? Please ask for proof of their sales stats and don't just take their word for it. If they don't have stats, ask for former employer references so you can confirm them yourself.

If at any time during the interview, you feel that the candidate is over-embellishing their qualifications or flat out lying to you, take that as a red flag and do a hard pass.

Take it from me. You don't want problems with this employee later on down the line. Trust your instincts.

If you feel that a candidate is vague in their answers, ask for more clarity. Don't be afraid to get it out in the open.

Remember, they are the face of your business. It is absolutely in your best interest to want to hire the best of the best for the positions you have available.

If it comes down to a final two, look at how well each candidate understands the industry and how long they have been in the industry.

Newbies tend to be more open to change in the marketplace because they don't have deep-seated roots and past experience with the negativity of the field. They are clean, so to speak, to mold and mentor to the new way of sales.

Keep in mind it's all about how they treat their customers at the end of the day, and if they can sell cars.

Services and Customer Service Excellence

Regardless of how much a buyer wants or loves a certain car, the sale is not going to happen if the cost is not right for them.

A few of the profitable ways you can enhance your dealership's customer approval and satisfaction rating include offering the convenience of mobile payments, a 24/7 customer support line, and live chat with the service department.

You can also elect to offer many other in-demand services related to helping your customers get the financing they need to get in the car they want and love.

Some of these include service agreements that go beyond the normal manufacturer's warranty coverage.

You may want to provide coverage for unlikely mechanical failure and even offer vehicle insurance policies, which are always handled through a licensed and reputable insurance company.

Offer Dealer Financing

Offering dealer financing is a distinctly profitable additional service to offer in your used auto dealership simply because it provides significant financial options for your potential buyer.

The lion's share of the negotiating more often than not happens right on the showroom floor among your finance department and your potential buyer. The loan amount is actually on behalf of a third party finance company based on standard pre-approval conditions and requirements.

This type of business model approach represents a nominal risk to you as the dealership and offers supreme benefit to the potential buyer. The buyer often ends up with a better rate using this particular financing method rather than trying to get a loan with their personal credit union or bank.

In addition to huge customer benefits already mentioned, you can take advantage of other perks for your customers.

The key to vehicle financing is that you, as the dealership, only handle the negotiating and offer the option. You have nothing to do with the actual financing as that is done strictly through a third party vendor.

All transactions beyond the initial introduction will remain between that third-party vendor and your buyer. This protects the integrity of the deal and privacy of your customers.

Have a Service Department

Think of your maintenance and repair department as an extension of the showroom floor.

It is an invaluable offering that will ultimately financially benefit the bottom line of the auto dealership while proving to be extremely advantageous to your potential buyers.

When a car dealership takes the proactive step to offer an expertly trained team of professionals and experts, it results in flawless vehicle care as well as fast and simple access to the parts they need to purchase.

Your customer will enjoy the gratification of knowing that their vehicles are in trusted, professional hands.

Just as equally rewarding for you is the increased profit margin you can experience by offering an expertly staffed and quality service department.

This is a great way to keep happy buyers coming back and upgrading and trading in their current vehicles for new models you obtain later on.

Service with a Smile

If you don't take anything else away from this section, I want you to know while it is your job and goal as a dealership owner to sell vehicles, it is likewise equally important for the customer to have a rewarding experience.

Giving customers this awesome experience means providing stellar customer service. This is the key to any service you offer to potential buyers.

Poor customer experience can stop a car sale dead in its tracks.

Something as simple as a smile will definitely help your used car dealership stand apart from the competition.

Not only are today's buyers much more sophisticated in their knowledge about the car buying process, but the overload of information found on the internet and the current state of the economy also makes buyers more cautious and rational with their major purchases.

Because of this, potential buyers and customers automatically come in the door with a higher expectation of a business' salesperson. This is both in terms of what they comprehend and how they want to receive the information.

Underestimating the significance of exceptional customer service can mean the difference between a potential customer walking out the door in under seven minutes flat or creating a mutually satisfying relationship that results in a sale.

Daily Tasks of a Used Car Dealership

While this sample day is not all-inclusive, it does encompass some of the most important tasks that you need to plan on working into your daily schedule. This routine will allow you to remain efficient in operating your business.

These steps are not listed in any order of particular importance but are rather a guideline for beneficial daily practice.

Analyze Sales

Break down and review all of your previous day's sales and analyze the types of cars that sold the most and to whom.

This is where you want to identify and document the common trends and buying patterns that happened during the previous day's sales. From that data, it's up to you to come up with a solid plan for replacing sold inventory.

Here is where you want to look at more details about the cars that were sold. There are some important questions to ask about the data you collect.

- How many days did the car sit on the lot before it was sold?
- Was the price you sold it for within market or industry range for that type of vehicle?
- What was your profit margin?
- How many more of that vehicle do you have left in your inventory?
- Where did you get this car? Was it purchased at an auction or a trade?

From the answers to these questions, examine if it makes the most sense to keep this type of car on your lot and to acquire more.

You may want to consider reaching out to other dealers to negotiate deals for their aging inventory, which match your core needs.

Simply locate cars already in the market that have been reconditioned and have a low market days supply.

The market days supply measures the scarcity of a particular make and model of a vehicle in the market. A higher market days supply means a greater number of competing units. They may be overpriced or poorly marketed by their current dealer.

Identify fast-moving vehicles in the marketplace on sites like CarandDriver.com (https://www.caranddriver.com/). Drill down into the current market listings. Identify aging units in the market and buy them wholesale before they go to auction.

Review Appraisals

Consult with your sales team, or do this yourself, to find out about the appraisals that were done the previous day.

Review past appraisals with your sales consultants to put a game plan together for recapturing potentially lost trades.

Host daily "save-a-deal" meetings to have another set of eyes look at your low-performing sales managers.

Examine Your Pricing Strategy

Consider your pricing strategy and make the necessary adjustments. Compile a game plan for executing this.

Here are a few recommended best practices for examining your pricing strategy.

Physically pull the keys to each car. Book it out, check market listings, open the car, start it, check the tires, and do a general walk-around.

After examining the cars, create an ultimatum. For example, when a car reaches a number of days old, re-evaluate its position in the market for pricing only when it hits this age.

If you are doing this every day, there will only be a handful of cars on the list.

It is imperative to give a car time to adjust to new pricing and have a chance to sell.

Be "in the game." Don't just look at a report to tell you the list of cars you are asking for above and below market average prices on, know why every car falls into each category.

Time to Market (TTM) Review

Review your "time to market" and the performance of your online ads and marketing.

Accelerate your time to market (TTM) by streamlining the process from appraisal through reconditioning (recon) and into online ads.

Follow up in your service drive to push cars through recon and get new inventory to market.

The recommended benchmark of TTM should take no more than 72 Hours. Actual time to market will vary based on the dealership.

Know your setup and benchmark based on your top-performing months and shoot for a 20% improvement each month.

Source New Inventory

Source for new inventory by attending live auctions or online wholesale shops that offer floor credit.

We discussed auctions at length in the previous chapter.

You may also want to consider running a "we buy cars" campaign to source more inventory.

To Franchise or Not to Franchise Part 2

We touched on this briefly earlier, but let's get down into the details.

I want to be crystal clear that there is no right or wrong when it comes to determining how you plan on starting your used auto dealership.

Essentially, you should be motivated by your overall business goals and vision with a clear and concise mission statement.

A franchised dealership is one that sells both new and pre-owned vehicles. This means that as a franchise, you would have a much broader selection of pre-owned vehicles than if you were to open your dealership independently.

The quality of the pre-owned vehicles and trucks at a franchise dealership tends to be better but a little older in make and model. What that means for you as the dealership is more of a profit margin on the vehicles you sell.

If you wish to start a used car dealership that primarily offers only newer cars, that also has a service department, and you want to open your doors with name-brand recognition already, then opening a franchise instead of an independent dealership is the best choice for you.

If you prefer to buy used vehicles from several different types of car manufacturers without the need to worry about exclusivity, then an independent car dealership might be the wiser option for you.

Operating an auto dealership franchise is an established platform where there are set regulations and rules exclusive to each individual manufacturer. By law, you must comply with these on the sale of each and every vehicle from your lot.

These restrictions are not necessary or existent in an independent dealership. If you crave that type of independence then a franchise option might not be the way to go.

Take your time and decide, there's no rush to get started, but it's a lot easier than having to change course mid-start-up which might delay your launch.

Chapter 5: Selling Cars

Times have changed. Long gone are the days where you could simply buy a building, run a few ads in the newspaper, make a radio appearance at the local radio station, put a sign out front, and talk to customers as they come in to inquire about your inventory.

In the old days, it only took a friendly disposition and a hometown atmosphere that made people feel safe and welcome to sell cars.

The well-oiled machine of yesteryear has come and gone. We no longer live in an analog world.

We've graduated to digital everything, and face-to-face social situations barely exist anymore due to receiving instant gratification from technology.

A customer can go on the internet and within a matter of minutes, find every single piece of information on a vehicle within 1,000 miles of them.

What that means for you is that a low price point is not even a guaranteed sale these days.

It's not about racing to the bottom with your pricing model. Nobody wants to engage with prices that are too low. It doesn't help your bottom line to sell a car below its value. Nobody wins in that situation.

Countering Tunnel Vision

Just as operating any other industry during fluctuating times in the 21st century, you are required to remain agile and open to new opportunities and possibilities that are hidden within each of the challenges you face.

Many of the potential buyers you encounter will already have a vehicle in mind. It's highly likely they have researched the car they want extensively. They have taken plenty of virtual tours of the vehicle and probably researched the car down to every last bolt and inspection.

Unfortunately, doing a lot of research and consuming an overflow of information on the web often leads to buyers having a sort of tunnel vision. This tunnel vision often makes it hard to get their mind to go in another direction even if it makes more sense financially and safety wise.

As the dealership, it's your job to determine what types of benefits and features your customers need or want in their car buying experience. Knowing this allows you to meet those needs and desires better.

For example, if your customer wants to purchase a specific model of vehicle that appears to be extremely fancy, you have the ability to offer them a model from your inventory that closely matches their description of their dream car.

Ask Open-Ended Questions

Ask open-ended questions. That's going to be the key to getting your tunnel vision buyer out of the fast and fancy mindset and consider other alternatives.

Don't ask your buyer if they want to purchase a fast car. The answer will obviously be yes, or you could get a blank stare.

Ask them instead, "If you didn't have to worry about the cost of the car, what would be your ultimate dream car?"

From that, you can determine how to help them get close to or exactly what they want depending on your inventory.

Asking open-ended questions of your buyers is a great way to break the ice and also bolster friendly conversation. This conversation starts chipping away at some of the initial tension and fear that new used car buyers are often haunted with.

Get on a Personal Level

Asking open-ended questions also allows your potential buyer to open up to you on a more personal level. Hopefully, they will start to share things with you and establish a level of trust.

The most critical point to keep in mind is that the human connection is what sets you apart from the other dealerships and your salespeople should be employing this tactic.

Let's examine the reasons for opening a used car dealership versus a new car dealership.

New or Used Vehicles

One would assume that having a new car dealership is where the big profits are. In some ways, you are right.

New cars are a high ticket item. New car sales make up more than half of the total gross sales at a new car dealership.

The average gross profit of a new car is around $2000 per vehicle. While that may seem like a nice little chunk of change, from a net-profit perspective, it's a loss.

The typical new car will cost a dealership roughly $200 per sale.

Commissions for new car salesman tend to be a little bit on the higher side.

Transparency in your pricing model with buyers and what's known in the industry as "floor planning" indicates that new cars are all sizzle and no steak for dealership owners.

Borrowing money and credit potentially from the car manufacturer is pretty much the only guaranteed funding source to get all of the vehicles on the showroom floor and into your inventory.

The longer a car remains on your lot, the more you have to pay interest on the loan. "Hold back" is what is referred to as small amounts of cash that the manufacturer kicks back to the dealer when the car finally does sell.

In general, there just is not a large amount of profit margin in new car sales. There is definitely cash flow coming into the business, but it's not a profit. There's a big difference.

It's equally important to examine the profits of selling used vehicles.

Examine the trade allowance that you used to acquire the vehicle in the first place and tack on the cost of fixing any repairs to get the vehicle back on the road or in quality condition as well as repairs that are not covered under warranty.

The longer used cars sit on your lot, the less they are worth. You can increase your profit margins by hiring relatively low commissioned yet experienced sales people with previous used car sales experience.

Studies conducted by the NADA (National Automobile Dealers Association) suggest that used vehicles typically remain on the lot about 45 days. It is also reported that if they do manage to sit on your lot for longer than that, you are typically losing sales, and those cars should be evaluated during your daily review.

Back in the day, the car dealership business was not quite as transparent as it is now.

The online "Kelly Blue Book" was actually a literal blue book you held in your hand and had three prices listed for each type of vehicle.

This price list included the low price, the wholesale price, and the retail price.

Back then, the price was subject to change based on the current condition of the vehicle.

An ideal situation for a dealer to offer a potential buyer would be the wholesale price as a trade.

Most dealerships tend to have car buyers lean towards a car purchase at the MSRP (Manufacturer's Suggested Retail Price) which is the ideal situation for a customer wanting a trade in.

You can buy a car at the wholesale price, fix it up if need be, then resell it at the MSRP creating a nice profit.

Next, we'll examine how to market and advertise your dealership.

Marketing and Advertising

Advertising can often be considered inconsistent at best, especially when trying to imagine a new and compelling idea.

That's why you typically see the same thing from every dealership to dealership across the country.

In order to stand out from the crowd, when sales don't come in back to back, it becomes even more of a challenge to keep the course and rejuvenate failed campaigns and slogans.

That's why I've put together a list of advertising ideas that helped save the day when I owned my used car dealership. Try a mixture of these ideas and stay consistent to drive sales up and give you a competitive advantage.

Build Partnerships

Local area businesses are your best asset, especially the ones who are your indirect competition but still connected closely to the customers you want to target.

Having multiple partner businesses in the community that promote your car dealership, and whose business you likewise promote, is a simple and clean way of getting the referrals through word of mouth.

These are customers they already do business wit, which means they already have an established relationship and trust built, so the recommendation holds more weight.

Word of mouth is extremely profitable. The relationship with your partner lets you know they are a serious buyer who isn't just a tire kicker.

When you partner with other area businesses and form a referral partnership, you cultivate your own word of mouth network where referrals are encouraged and found useful among the group.

A side note to this strategy is that you need to implement this advertising idea with caution and make sure you are partnering with a reputable business who will actually send you a reciprocal referral. There's nothing worse than a one-sided referral relationship.

Be Unorthodox

Car buyers have certain expectations of their car dealerships. Unfortunately, not everything they're expecting is great.

Regardless of whether we like it or not, as dealerships, we have some negative stereotypes in the industry that have been hard to escape from.

Misleading car prices, commission-driven salespeople, high-pressure choices, strong-arm tactics, and more have tainted dealership's reputations.

I am in no way trying to scare you or discourage you from perusing your dream. I deeply apologize for bringing up these distressing and often untrue or over exaggerated car dealer stereotypes, but I have a good reason for doing so.

What can you do to deal with and overcome the stereotypes that exist?

Market and advertise your dealership and yourself as the owner they will trust in a way that rebukes the industry stereotypes. Do this not just with rhetoric but with action.

Be honest and straightforward with your customers in your marketing. Make everything no-pressure sales.

While trying too hard to be different and live up to an expectation or image, you can actually end up perpetuating the stereotypes.

I've seen it happen to the best of the best in this business.

With that being said, feel free to be as unorthodox as you can while maintaining integrity. You will be amazed at how many repeat and excited car buyers you will see walk through your front doors.

Create a Website

Your website is the virtual showroom floor for your inventory.

A website can be a digital business card for your dealership. It will be where people can go to get your address, see your specials and sales, and read your testimonials.

A dealership's website will be part of the customer's extensive research process. You can choose to showcase your best deals or to push cars that have a longer market days analysis.

Gather Testimonials

I've previously mentioned the power of word of mouth marketing and advertising.

Testimonials from happy customers and buyers are huge for social proof or credibility for your business.

Surprisingly, they are extremely easy to obtain from customers once you have helped them get into the car they love and need. It just requires you asking them!

Happy customers will be your most valuable resource in this business. Getting them to comment on your buying process and your dealership and how you rebuke the typical car dealership stereotypes is gold.

There are a few approaches you can take when asking for a customer testimonial. How you do it depends on your preference and the customers you primarily serve.

You can ask them to complete a quick online survey set up through SurveyMonkey.com or a similar site at the end of the sale while they are still in your presence and happy.

Ideally, it's best to get the testimonial or survey in their hands before they even leave your lot.

Ask them their overall impression of your business, the employees, and your online presence.

If you are tech-savvy like me, you can create QR codes that people can scan at your various departments and leave reviews from their mobile phone.

Make sure you have properly groomed your staff on how to handle asking for a testimonial and feedback. It's all about having them take pride and ownership of their hard work and conveying that to the customer in the form of feedback.

Customers want to be kept happy and your staff asking what they can do to improve and keep them happy will go a long way.

You can also take time to do follow up calls with all of your closed sales and ask them opinions later if you aren't comfortable doing it at the close of the sale.

Ask them if the car is still to their satisfaction. Let them know of your referral incentives for the month and how they can benefit from sending customers your way. Offer them discounts on their parts and service or specials on future trade-ins.

Regardless of how you get the testimonial data, once you have them, it's important to let the world know. Post them on your social media pages, add a testimonial page to your website, and absolutely include them in any and all of your marketing and advertising materials.

Car shoppers love to purchase a car from an establishment that has positive and consistent reviews because that's part of their fact-finding and discovery phase of the buying process.

Try creative ways to reward customers for their review, and remember, to always ask!

Get Refreshed on Social Media Tactics

It's no secret that dealerships aren't the most social media savvy bunch in the world. I'm probably an exception to the rule just because of my curiosity and trying to keep up with my grandchildren.

One of those stereotypes about car dealerships that rings on the true side is that their social media pages and ads tend to be full of spam and tacky looking.

The majority of car buyers who are social media users are not interested in looking at every single vehicle you have online. They also don't want to see ads to the same car on their timeline or newsfeed 20 times a day. That's quite unprofessional.

On the flip side, social media can be a little too personal, and that is when things get awkward.

People do not follow "Joe's Car Dealership" to see posts about the community garden's cucumber that looks like Donald Duck.

Social media should be relevant but not narrow-minded. Show something about your personality and business besides just cars.

Be funny yet tactful. Your customers are not your close circle of your friends and family.

While you can always get a ton of attention on social media these days just getting it wrong, you don't want to be that dealership.

Find a mix of funny yet engaging content posts that show how your dealership is the strength of the community and what value you bring.

After all, people make the business, not the cars.

Host Events to Market Trade-ins

Trade-ins are a great way for you to become integrated with the community your dealership is a part of.

Host a car-wash or community event and offer people a trade-in.

You can do events in the winter time to entice people to come in the door. Offer free tire rotation or weatherization inspections, have disaster checks for safety, and host charity events like canned food or toy drives while serving hot chocolate. As they drive through and drop off their donations, hand them a cup of hot cocoa and a flyer about trade-in specials and or service rewards and offerings.

Summer concerts are a great way to drive traffic to your lot. They can be a relatively inexpensive way of marketing and advertising while also bringing the community together.

Make sure you keep the pitch neutral because you have gotten them there under one pretense with the intention of adding another one when they arrive.

These are the marketing ideas that got me through my best times as a car dealership owner.

All great ideas must be immediately followed by action. Get out there and put these ideas into practice and reap your increased profits!

Legal Considerations

Car buyers who purchase a used vehicle are protected under federal law.

The law applies to every used car dealership or seller who intends to sell six or more used cars during a year's timeframe.

As we discussed, used cars are those that have been previously owned and driven more than the sparse mileage incurred when doing a test drive or lot move.

Maine and Wisconsin are currently exempt from this law. The reason for this is because these two particular states have incorporated a comprehensive protection plan for used car buyers on the state level. It makes the federal laws redundant.

Any dealership that does not obey these federal laws will be subject to fines penalties and even potential civil lawsuits.

I'm going to share with you the basic legal requirements for your used car dealership to be legally compliant in the United States.

Buyer's Guide

You are required to display a buyer's guide in the window of each vehicle on your lot. This buyer's guide must contain the warranty details that are currently offered at the state level as well as any additional provisions and protections that the buyer is afforded under federal law.

Your displayed buyer's guides must have the following components and sections to be compliant:

Mandatory Disclosures

Your displayed buyer's guide must include these mandatory disclosures:

- The 14 major systems of a car along with the potential defects that can occur in each one

- A suggestion to the consumer regarding asking the dealer if pre-purchase inspections are allowed

- A warning that the buyer cannot rely on any spoken promises by the dealer that aren't confirmed in writing

- The car make, model, and the year the car was manufactured

- The VIN of the vehicle or some type of vehicle identification number

Warranty Information

All warranty details and information must be in your buyer's guide and include the warranties that you as the dealer and the buyer agree to during negotiations of the car sale.

If the car is used and still under the manufacturer's warranty, then your buyer guide must state that.

It must also contain the following warranty information:

- Whether a warranty is full or limited

- Percentage of cost a seller will pay under the warranty

- Specific systems covered by the warranty

- Duration of the warranty

- The name, address, and telephone number of the person that handles warranties for the seller

- Language that informs the buyer that they might have rights not shown on the warranty

State Used Car Laws

State laws, much like federal laws, are designed to provide consumers with protections against predatory sellers who don't have good intentions.

That's not you.

Nevertheless, it's still required to be included in your buyer's guide.

Your state will require that you be specific about the protections your buyers have in terms of the vehicle working for a certain amount of time or up to a certain mileage after the sale.

There are four categories of warranties that are recognized as standard. The main one that you will need to worry about as a used car dealer is the "As Is" warranty.

Please do your research on what other specific warranties your state requires.

As-Is Warranty Declaration

The "as is" warranty is primarily required in states where there are no formal laws in place to protect consumers. These laws are also referred to as "lemon laws."

That means if you buy a used car today and then it stops working tomorrow, you essentially have no type of recourse without any lemon laws in place.

Due to the high potential for consumer abuse of the law, the "as is" warranty exists in some states.

The "as-is" warranty states that as long as the dealer discloses that there is no warranty provided with the vehicle, their liability is limited later down the line.

Please look up the lemon laws in your state and also the requirements for "as is" warranty disclosures.

There are many legal considerations when operating and starting a used car dealership. Please do your research and make sure you are complying with all federal and state requirements.

Let's talk about a nontraditional sales approach to selling the cars on your lot now that you know what you need to do to be compliant.

Flipping Cars

My early family memories involve selling baseball cards at the local flea market and traveling to auto auctions with my father and Uncle Sam.

I was an adult at the time but felt like a kid on his way to the circus.

I still recall how exciting it was when they invited me to go with them to my first car auction.

I became captivated by all of the action happening between the auctioneer and the people with the paddles.

My Uncle Sam's voice cut through the bidding to yell the winning bid for a beat-up and rusted yet supposedly reliable pick-up truck.

Three weeks and two paint jobs later, I was able to watch him sell it for a $3,500 profit.

I was immediately hooked.

That was almost 15 years ago, and I've been flipping cars aside from running my used car dealership in my spare time ever since. My quickest flip to date was a short six hours.

Sam taught me that there are two types of auctions. There's the auto dealer exclusive auctions and public auctions.

I personally favored public auctions merely because they sold the exact same types of vehicles the dealer-only auctions sold but without the dealer license requirements.

Each state has its own set of rules relating to auctions. In my state, if you are over the age of 18, you are able to bid on any type of vehicle you wish even when competing against many other qualified bidders. This gave me the ability to acquire a vehicle well below retail value.

I also used Craigslist a lot to find great used car deals. Craigslist listings are categorized by city or region so you can conveniently search in your immediate area.

There are literally hundreds if not thousands of new daily listings. Craigslist is free to use, which makes it an absolute goldmine of a resource.

Through the years I have figured out how to consistently generate thousands of dollars on each used car I was able to flip, but I eventually ran into a problem.

Two years into flipping cars, I began to notice that I was spending way too much time trying to find deals on the internet.

The research was a buzz-kill, believe me.

I was literally obsessed with finding inventory. It consumed almost all of my free time.

Was I making a profit? Sure. But was it really worth all of the time I was putting into it?

I knew there had to be an easier way to get this done, which led me to ask myself a serious question.

What was the most amount of time I was willing to devote to the process of finding inventory and then actually buying and selling the vehicle?

At the time, I had no idea what the answer was, but it was my mission to find out.

Let me share that answer with you so you can save yourself some heartache down the line.

Plan on Purchasing to Flip

Keeping the flip in mind enables you to keep a good profit margin. I've been able to acquire good used cars for as little as $500; it just takes time to locate those deals.

Factor in repair costs. You must repair the vehicle and have it inspected in order to make it roadworthy and to sell it.

You will also want to have the car cleaned and detailed. For some of the cars you acquire, it merely means a little soap and water. For many others, it may require a new transmission or engine.

Repairs of that magnitude give me pause. It's wise to evaluate if there's enough of a profit after repairs when going this route.

Consider advertising and marketing. I highly encourage you to stick with what works and what is mostcost-effective. So far, nothing has beat Craigslist when it comes to flipping cars. It only takes a few minutes to post, and the replies are endless.

Now comes the good part - the actual flipping of the car.

One of the most valuable lessons I learned about flipping cars was that the most important part of the process, which is finding the vehicles, was almost the most time-consuming.

Nearly 80% of my time was spent on merely trying to identify a great value and a good car.

I came up with a foolproof way of having the deals fall in my lap instead of me chasing them down.

It actually worked.

Here's what worked for me when I got it right.

Use a Craigslist Search Tool App

CraigslistPro (CPRO) is one of the many Craigslist companion apps for your smartphone. You can download the app right to your Android or other smartphone, and it allows you to get instant alerts from Craigslist. You can search for any new listings that match your specific criteria.

I typically set mine to send me alerts and push notifications at any given time for any ad containing the words "priced to sell," "make an offer," or "must sell quick," in the vehicle category.

People who need to sell their vehicle quick are more apt to do so at a deal and using an app allows you to see those deals before anyone else does.

There is a free and paid version of the CPRO app, and the free version is all you need to get started but with limited alerts.

Search your app store for your device to use a similar Craigslist alert and search app.

Wanted Ads on Craigslist

These aren't your granny's wanted ads.

Target your ads specifically to people who want a quick sale which usually translates into a great deal for you.

The great part is wanted ads on Craigslist are 100% free.

Here's an example of an ad that I have used before.

Ad Title:"I want a car today. I have CASH"

Ad Description:"I'm looking for a reliable vehicle ASAP. I have $2,500 CASH, and I can pick it up today. Text or call with what you have to [my phone number]."

Pay to Play

Every single person on this planet knows of someone who is either considering purchasing a car or selling one.

I used that to my advantage and offered everyone I knew a finder's fee. A finder's fee means that, for example, if they sent me a $3,000 referral for a car flip, I would give them $300 as their fee.

In this example, the finder's fee is about 10% of the sales amount. You are free to set your finder's fee to whatever amount you feel comfortable.

It can be a percentage, or it can be a set amount of money. A good rule of thumb is 5-10% of the sales price or of the profits.

Your finder's fee can also be a set amount of money no matter what the price is of the sale. For instance, you can offer $100 flat to anyone who brings you a referral.

That money was a great motivator for people to send their friends and co-workers my way constantly.

Profit and Commission Structures

Car auctions have always been the best source of inventory for finding used cars.

Auctions are quick and the cars you find there are reasonably priced. They also offer additional services like reports and dealer only trade-ins.

What I tend to be wary of at auctions are the cars that look dirty. Why? Because people avoid these cars like the plague because they assume it's a wreck.

This isn't always a good move. Sure, it absolutely could be a lemon, but more often than not, it belonged to someone who never parked it in the garage or maybe didn't drive it often. It could have been parked under some trees for all we know, and the owner just didn't bother to clean it off.

Case Study Example of a Profit

I bought a 15-year-old Volvo at an auction 5 years ago for $350. I was the only one brave enough to bid on it.

There were hundreds of bidders there that day. The Volvo happened to be among a slew of other vehicles. It had a flat tire and dark paint which made it look extraordinarily dull and bad on the eyes. It looked like it was just plain old tired.

When I went over to open the driver's side door of the car, I noticed fast food wrappers and a slew of other garbage throughout the vehicle. Crazy enough, there was no odor.

It was later revealed this was a repossession. The dealer who originally wanted it back must have taken one single look at that dirty car with the flat tire and decided to try to recover some losses by sending it straight to the auction.

What an amazing find! A diamond in the rough!

I turned the ignition over and did my usual mental checklist. I could not find one single thing wrong.

Now keep in mind I had not driven it anywhere yet and wouldn't be able to because of the flat tire. It didn't really matter to me. The car started, and I was knowledgeable enough to know that I was going to be able to make a decent profit after repairs at this price.

As I ran through my final check, I actually felt myself holding my breath. I took out a handkerchief from my pocket and wiped it on the rear bumper of the car. To my surprise, it actually revealed a shine. Bingo!

I got the car towed to my dealership garage, and I had the repair department get to work. The first thing they did was clean off the engine, rims, and tires to see a clear picture of the shape of the body of the car.

It was beautiful.

I had them focus on the outside first. They buffed it down, polished it like a shoe, and repaired the flat tire.

Now at this time Volvos of this quality and age were selling for about $7,000-$8,000.

I just paid $350. I immediately sold the car by advertising it in my local newspaper for a quick $7,500.

It was never about holding out and stalling to get that highest price for me. It was bought by an elderly couple who were completely thrilled to have it.

They wanted it for safety reasons and of course its record of reliability. That made me proud. Moments like those will let you know it's all worth it in the end.

I already had my dealership established when I started flipping cars.

For those of you starting out, however, flipping cars can create the funding you need for your business to become a licensed and fully operational used car dealership.

Flipping cars is a great way to start without a large investment of time or money, and it's pretty straight-forward.

Flipping cars gives you a little bit of freedom to operate legally as a consumer who can buy and sell as many cars as you want throughout any given year.

This strategy allows you to work from home, or wherever you are most comfortable, and you won't have to incur any overhead like a traditional dealership.

Back End Commission

Used car buyers typically tend to care more about the cost than they do when they are purchasing a new vehicle. A new vehicle can come fully loaded with all the latest bells and whistles.

Here is the fact of the matter - if all dealerships sold new cars, there would no longer be any car dealerships.

What may be surprising for you to learn is that car dealers don't typically get rich off selling cars. There's not much of a profit margin. Now, don't run off screaming just yet. Hear me out.

So if in fact, dealers lose profit during car sales, after figuring in expenditures and overhead, then how can you possibly create a successful and profitable used car dealership?

The short answer is what is called "back-end commission." This is the secondary source of profit for a car dealership.

The "front end commission" is what is made on the initial sale of the car. As you can then infer, the "back end commission" is what is made after the sale of the vehicle along with everything sold after it.

What does this mean? Let's look at a real-life example to explain how this works.

Let's say that you go to an auction and purchase a car for $19,000 and sell it for $20,000.

You have made an instant $1,000 profit in "front end commission." That's just where things get started.

After the customer has purchased the vehicle, your finance manager, which is one of the key employees you should have in your organization, will then take them back to their office for the long and grueling task of filling out paperwork, securing financing, and completing a myriad of other tasks.

If that customer chooses to use your financing that is part of the aforementioned "other things sold after the car."

A dealership can make anywhere from an additional $1,000 - $5,000. If the customer chooses your preferred insurance company, or extended services and warranties, you can earn additional revenue from that sale as well.

It's best to establish relationships with companies that offer you great incentives for repeat business or volume business. There are plenty out there, and this essentially is a win/win situation.

It should be easy to find companies willing to work with you to secure financing, insurance, or additional services and warranties for your customers.

Chapter 6: The Customer Viewpoint

Dealer Financing

Dealer financing has some advantages.

For starters, it's convenient. It's possible to finance your car and drive it home the same day, whereas it may take a few days for a bank or credit union to process your application for an auto loan.

A dealership may be less stringent than a traditional lender in terms of credit approval, making access to a loan easier for buyers with lower credit scores.

There's a potential catch. In exchange for financing, the dealer may charge a higher interest rate or loan origination fee, both of which increase the cost of buying.

For example, according to Experian, used car buyers with subprime credit paid an average interest rate of

15.7% (rising to 17.6% from independent car dealers) for a car loan in 2016.

Buyers with deep subprime credit paid even more, with an interest rate averaging 19.03%. Higher rates translate to a higher monthly payment and more money spent over the loan term.

If you have a better credit rating, a bank or credit union may be a preferred source for a used car loan.

Start with the financial institution that holds your checking and savings accounts. If you already have a history with a particular bank or credit union, it may be willing to give you a discount on the interest rate or fees for a loan.

Customer Leasing Versus Purchasing

Here's something that a lot of people don't realize - you can lease used cars!

Many consumers assume leasing is only for new cars. What they overlook is that leasing is simply an alternative method of financing.

Leasing works exactly the same with a used car as it does with a new car. The main difference is that your monthly lease payment will likely be much less.

The biggest part of a lease payment is attributed to depreciation cost. Since cars depreciate heavily during the first 2 to 3 years, it makes sense to take advantage of the situation by leasing a used car and taking a smaller hit on the depreciation.

The only problem is that many banks and financing companies stopped providing used car leasing in the wake of the financial crisis in 2008.

Since then, only a few players have tip-toed back into this market. You may have a hard time finding a company that will provide leasing on a used car.

A customer's best bet may be to look into leasing a certified pre-owned car through a dealership. The dealership can try to arrange the lease through one of its finance partners or through a credit union. Another alternative is to try an independent leasing company such as LeaseCompare.com.

Conclusion

Car dealerships and used car dealerships, in particular, are one of the only business models remaining that has not, nor can it truly ever be, replaced by a massive e-commerce industry.

One of the main reasons is that people need more from the car buying experience than a nice website or pictures online. A click of the button, or drop and drag to cart is not at all an effective or realistic way to sell cars.

Car salesmen have to be therapists, educators, and extended family all rolled into one. Customers also want to be able to test drive their potential investment.

They want to see how your facility operates in terms of service. Do you offer service with a smile?

They lean on your expertise to become educated about making the best decision for their family, their budget, and their lifestyle.

I've seen many car dealerships come and go in my long career. What has remained consistent among the dealerships that are still around is that they have repeat customers and quality inventory.

While this is not the industry that it was 30 years ago when I got started, one thing has remained tried and true.

In the used car sales industry, used car sales are a formidable force to be reckoned with.

The market has never been better for individuals who are striving to begin their own used car dealership.

Used car dealerships are a recession sturdy business model, with stock on the rise consistently at 3.5% month after month.

If you have a passion for cars, helping others, and making lots of money, you cannot go wrong with starting your own car dealership.

If you are a former salesman, you bring skills to the table that will ensure your success for long-term viability in the market. Tap into that.

Likewise, if you are a mechanic, you are also a perfect candidate to start your own car dealership. You know a lot about automobiles, you typically already have an established customer base, and you will know where to get parts and equipment as needed at below cost.

As you contemplate your options, think about if you want to join an existing dealership franchise or if you want to be an independent brand of your own. Either way is fine. There is no right or wrong answer, but it must be one that is realistic for your current circumstances and finances.

If you choose to become an independent brand, you are going to need to do extensive market research. This research is part of your business plan, anyway.

Determine what your competitors in the area are doing and whether you are going to be able to meet and hopefully exceed their current standards to better position yourself in the market.

Location is most important and not just for your brick and mortar location.

Your online presence is equally important. Do not skimp on proper website design.

You need a custom-made website that is easy to navigate, visually appealing, and provides value to your visitors. Your website is your virtual showroom floor for your inventory.

As a used car dealership, you have the advantage of picking and choosing only inventory you know is selling and in demand. New car dealerships are forced to stock their floors with the latest trend and not necessarily the better value or best quality.

To ensure you are actually selling cars, you need to understand your local area and demographics.

For example, if you live in a rural area, you probably don't want to stock your lot with convertibles. In this case, you may lean more towards back country road vehicles and SUVs.

Make sure your lot is on a flat piece of land and is zoned for commercial use.

You will need to keep impeccably detailed documents for your licensure process. You can obtain these documents at your local state Department of Motor Vehicles.

Before you are able to obtain your licensure, most states are going to require you to take a written test, complete your application, and pay your application fee. These requirements vary by state. You can see each state's requirements listed in the Appendix.

Make sure that your particular state doesn't require that you also own the deed to your lot if you are renting a lot space. Some states require having the deed as a way to discourage nonbusiness owners from purchasing commercial lots.

After you get your licensure, make sure to obtain your surety bond with a minimum of $25,000 in coverage. Again, each state has a minimum requirement that will protect any potential customers from bad sales by deceitful sellers.

In some states, these surety bonds expire, which means you will need to pay to have them renewed upon expiring to remain legally compliant.

Be sure you take time to research and attend the local auctions in your area, specifically wholesale auctions. These auctions will allow you to diversify your inventory with various automakers for a wider selection of cars for your clients. Keep in mind what is appropriate for your geographical location.

You can also take a look at the paper and find estate sales and closed or private auctions where you can obtain more vehicles.

In addition to reaching out and establishing a relationship with your local community, reach out to your local banker and ask them for a meeting.

During the meeting, establish yourself as the premiere and primary used car dealer in the area. Ask them to be the primary lender that you refer new customers to who need financing.

Ask them for ways they can help speed up the purchase process for your buyers, and if you can have a stack of loan applications, business cards, flyers, and frequently asked questions.

Remember, find ways to stand out from the competition. From the services you offer to the people you hire.

Make sure your auto mechanic and the person you hire for sales are more than equipped to relieve you of stress and not add more to it.

Find ways to create local buzz. Use colorful and attractive signs, streamers, and sidewalk art. If you feel you can expand outside of your local area, then consider all the alternatives.

Regardless of what you decide, make sure it's based on realistic expectations and you will have a successful and long lasting used car dealership.

Here's to your massive success!

Thank you so much for reading this book. I hope it has been extensively helpful to you while you begin this grand endeavor.

I greatly appreciate you buying this book. You have fulfilled my need for giving back and mentoring the next generation of used car dealers.

I hope this book has been a benefit for you. If it has, would you kindly consider leaving a review wherever you purchased this book?

It would help me to continue to spread my knowledge to other aspiring entrepreneurs.

Thank you and best of luck on your business journey!

Appendix: Regulations Listed by State

Alabama

A car dealer license is required by any person, corporation, or partnership who sells vehicles for retail or wholesale purposes. The limit is 5 or more vehicles in 12 months.

1. Apply for a tax number through the Alabama Revenue Site.
2. Complete an application for an Alabama Car Dealer License through the Alabama Department of Revenue Motor Vehicle Division.
3. Provide photos of the location and signs that meet the Alabama code.
4. Have the following insurance:
5. $50,000 bodily injury/accident
    a. $25,000 bodily injury/accident/person
    b. $25,000 property damage/accident
    c. $75,000/accident combined single limit
2. Pay the $25 fee.

3. Purchase a car dealer bond in the amount of $25,000.

4. Submit the following to the Alabama Department of Revenue:

   a. Transmittal sheet

   b. Original copy of the bond

   c. Insurance certification form

   d. Copy of a government ID for each business owner

   e. Pictures of the location and sign for your dealership

The renewal period is October 1st to September 30th.

Alaska

Anyone selling vehicles in Alaska needs to obtain a dealer's license.

1. Purchase a car dealer bond in the amount of $50,000 or just $25,000 if you are only selling motorcycles.

2. File an application for a license through the State of Alaska Division of Motor Vehicles.

3. Pay the $50 fee.

Licenses are good for 2 years after issuance.

Arizona

There are two types of licenses for standard dealerships and wholesalers.

1. Complete the application.
2. Get a criminal record check for anyone who owns over 20% of the company.
3. Purchase a bond in the amount of $100,000.
4. Submit the following to the Arizona Motor Vehicle Division:
   a. Application
   b. Original bond
   c. Fingerprints

Arkansas

An auto dealer license is required if you sell five or more vehicles in a calendar year.

1. Complete the application for an Arkansas Used Car Dealer License.
2. Purchase a bond in the amount of $25,000.
3. Submit the following to the Arkansas State Police attention Used Motor Vehicles:
   a. Application
   b. Original bond
   c. $250 fee

Licenses are good for one year.

California

A California Dealer License is required for anyone selling vehicles.

1. Complete an application.
2. Pay $176 application fee for a background check and fingerprinting.
3. Purchase a bond in the amount of $50,000.
4. Obtain a copy of the following:
   a. Proof of dealer education completion and pass a written exam.
   b. A copy of your rental or lease agreement.

    c. Signed and dated pictures of your business.

    d. A copy of your city or county business license and Certificate of Occupancy or Tax Certificate.

    e. A copy of your Board of Equalization Resale Permit.

5. Submit everything to the California DMV along with the following fees:

    a. $175 initial license application fee

    b. $1 Family Support Program fee

    c. $100 Auto broker fee

    d. $71 per dealer plate

Licenses are good for a year.

Colorado

A dealer license is required if you plan to sell more than three vehicles in a calendar year.

1. Ensure you meet the following requirements:

    a. The net worth of at least $100,000.

    b. Experian vantage score of at least 701.

    c. Pass a criminal background check.

2. Complete an application.
3. Gather the following information:
    a. Addendum for each member, owner, or partner.
    b. Copy of photo ID for each person that completed an addendum.
    c. Pre-licensing Education Certificate.
    d. Mastery Examination Affidavit.
    e. Affidavit of Restriction of Public Benefits for all owners.
    f. Statement of Financial Condition for the applicant and owners.
    g. Dealer Plate Affidavit.
    h. Business plan.
    i. Photographs of location.
    j. Sales tax license.
4. Purchase a bond in the amount of $50,000.
5. Pay the fee of $455.
6. Submit all the above paperwork and the original bond to the Department of Revenue Auto Industry Division.

The licensing period runs from July 1st to June 30th.

Connecticut

Anyone selling vehicles in Connecticut is required to get a license.

1. Get prerequisite approval of your location through the Zoning Board Chairman.
2. Meet the following state requirements:
    a. Have space to display and store at least two vehicles.
    b. Prove your repair department can hold at least two vehicles.
    c. Have a parts department and a business office for customers.
    d. Have at least one qualified mechanic.
    e. Have a wastewater retention tank with a minimum size of 250 gallons.
3. Complete an application.
4. Complete the following additional requirements:
    a. Application for Inspection.
    b. Application for Dealer Plates.
    c. Articles of Incorporation or Owner Information.
    d. An application fee of $140.

e. Sales tax permit number.

   f. Proof of insurance.

   g. Criminal History Record Request Form.

5. Purchase a bond in the amount of $50,000.

6. Submit all of the above documents to the Regulated Business Licensing Unit.

7. Pay the license fee of $560.

8. Pay for your plate fees of $140 registration per vehicle and $5 safety fee per plate.

Licenses are good for two years.

Delaware

Anyone selling vehicles in Delaware is required to get a license. You must sell at least five vehicles a year to maintain your license.

1. Complete an application.

2. Get a Criminal History Background Check and a Signature Authorization.

3. Meet the following requirements:

   a. Office with a desk and filing cabinets on premises.

   b. A business sign that is a minimum of 24"x36" and clearly visible from the road.

   c. A display lot large enough for five vehicles.

   d. An installed business telephone.

   e. A zoning approval form.

4. Purchase liability insurance.

5. Purchase a bond in the amount of $25,000.

6. Pay the licensing fee of $100 and $10 per each dealer tag.

7. Submit your application to the Delaware Department of Motor Vehicles.

8. Have your business location inspected

Licenses expire on December 31st of each year and renewal requires a record of all vehicles sold in the last year.

Florida

Anyone selling three or more vehicles in a year for retail purposes needs to get a license. All vehicles need to be titled in your name.

1. Have your dealership location approved by the DMV Compliance Examiner.
2. Complete an application.
3. Submit a fee of $300.
4. Purchase a bond in the amount of $25,000.
5. Provide proof of ownership or a copy of your lease.
6. Submit a garage liability insurance certificate that needs to include the following:
   a. $25,000 combined single limit liability coverage
   b. A bodily injury and property damage protection
   c. $10,000 personal injury protection
7. Provide a copy of registration or business.
8. Submit a copy of corporate papers or meeting notes.
9. Get a Sales Tax Number from the State of Florida Department of Revenue.
10. Submit your Federal Employer Identification Number.
11. Submit your fingerprints along with a fee of $54.25 a person.

12. Submit your application and copies of everything to the Florida Department of Highway Safety and Motor Vehicles.

All licenses expire on April 30th of each year. The cost of renewal is $75. Eight hours of continuing education is also required.

Georgia

If you sell five or more vehicles in a 12 month period, you need an auto dealer license.

1. Complete an application.
2. Attend a pre-licensing seminar.
3. Provide an original certificate of insurance.
4. Establish a location with a telephone line and photos of the location and signs.
5. Get a sales tax ID number through the Department of Revenue.
6. Purchase a bond in the amount of $35,000.
7. Submit a fingerprint-based criminal background check along with a $52.75 processing fee.
8. Pay the application fee of $170.

9. Mail everything to the Georgia State Board of Registration of Used Motor Vehicle Dealers.

Licenses are valid for two years and expire on March 31st of even-numbered years.

Hawaii

Sell at least 3 vehicles in one calendar year.

1. Be sure your location is approved with its respective county zoning ordinance.
2. Pay the fee, which ranges between $221-1172 depending on your county, island, whether it's new or used cars, and which year you apply.
3. Complete the dealer license application packet.
4. Submit the following items:
    a. A completed license application (Form 1016R)
    b. A self-inspection report
    c. Photographs of your business location
    d. Rental or lease agreement if you don't own the property.
    e. Proof of line of credit or a surety bond.
    f. A current financial statement

g. Proof of registration with the Hawaii BREG (Business Registration)

Renewed on or before June 30th of each even-numbered year.

Idaho

Anyone who sells five or more vehicles in a year is required to get a license.

1. Complete an application.
2. Pay the fee of $190, including $20.74 per dealer plate.
3. Complete pre-licensing education.
4. Purchase a bond in the amount of $20,000.
5. Submit your application to the Idaho Department of Transportation.
6. Have your location inspected

Licenses expire one year after issuance. The cost of renewal is $175.

Illinois

If you sell more than five vehicles in a 12 month period, you will need to get a license.

1. Complete an application.
2. Purchase a bond in the amount of $50,000.
3. Purchase an insurance policy that has the minimum:
   a. $100,000 for bodily injury
   b. $300,000 per accident
   c. $50,000 for property damage
4. Meet the following additional requirements:
   a. Provide a copy of your lease.
   b. Pass local zoning.
   c. Prove that your business is in good standing.
   d. Provide a Hazard Waste Generator Number.
5. Get a criminal background check.
6. Take an eight-hour training course.
7. Submit everything to the Secretary of State's Office Vehicle Services Department.
8. Pay the fee of $1,000. A master set of dealer plates is $45 with duplicates for $13.

Licenses expire on December 31st of each year.

Indiana

You need a license if you plan to sell over 12 vehicles in a year.

1. Complete an application.
2. Get a criminal background check.
3. Purchase a bond in the amount of $25,000.
4. Have insurance that includes the minimum:
    a. $100,000 bodily injury
    b. $300,000 bodily injury per accident
    c. $50,000 property damage
5. Provide the following additional requirements:
    a. Zoning approval
    b. Retail Merchant Certificate
    c. Federal Tax ID Number
6. Submit everything to the Office of the Indiana Secretary of State Auto Dealer Services Division.
7. Pay the $30 processing fee.

Iowa

If you are selling more than five vehicles in a 12 month period, you need to get a license.

1. Establish a place of business and pass zoning.
2. Pass an on-site inspection.
3. Purchase a bond in the amount of $75,000.
4. Complete an application.
5. Take an 8-hour pre-licensing course.
6. Submit everything to the Office of Vehicle Services Iowa Department of Transportation.

Licenses are good for 2 years and expire on December 31st of even-numbered years.

Kansas

Anyone selling vehicles in Kansas needs to get a license.

1. Meet the following initial requirements:
   a. Establish a place of business.
   b. Purchase liability and property damage insurance.

c. Prove tax clearance.

2. Purchase a bond in the amount of $30,000.

3. Complete your application.

4. Submit everything to the Kansas Department of Revenue Division of Motor Vehicles.

Licenses expire on December 31st of the year they were issued. The cost of renewal is $75.

Kentucky

There are 10 different types of dealer licenses in Kentucky. The requirements vary depending on which license you want.

1. Complete an Application
2. Obtain proof of approval from your city or county zoning authority
3. Your business name must clearly indicate that you are a motor vehicle dealership
4. Submit photographs and a detailed drawing of the location
5. Submit a financial statement
6. Give the state your tax permit number
7. Obtain liability insurance

a. $250,000 per 1 person

b. $500,000 per 1 occurrence

c. $250,000 for property damage

8. If selling new cars, obtain and submit a franchise agreement

9. Pay the fee

a. $100 dealer license

b. $40 application fee

c. $20 criminal background check per owner, partner, and corporate officer

Louisiana

If you sell over 4 vehicles in a 12 month period, you need to get a license.

1. Complete an application.
2. Complete a salesperson application.
3. Purchase a bond in the amount of $50,000.
4. Purchase garage liability insurance.
5. Get a zoning verification form.
6. Complete the following requirements:

a. Install a business phone.

b. Submit pictures of your location and signs.

    c. Complete an Educational Training Seminar Registration form

7. Pay the following licensing fees:

    a. $400 license fee

    b. $25 salesperson license

8. Submit everything to the Louisiana Used Motor Vehicle Commission.

Licenses are good for 2 years. There is a $100 fee for late renewals.

Maine

If you sell more than 5 vehicles in a year, you need to get a license.

1. Complete an application and include the following:

    a. Lease Form

    b. Plot Plan

    c. Land Use and Zoning Form

    d. Applicant Questionnaire

    e. Pass a background check

2. Submit everything to the Maine Bureau of Motor Vehicles with a $150 filing fee.

3. Pass a site inspection.
4. Purchase a bond in the amount of $25,000 if you won't sell over 50 vehicles a year.
5. Purchase garage liability insurance.

Licenses expire on the last day of the month one year from issuance. The cost of renewal is $150.

Maryland

If you sell vehicles in the state of Maryland, you will need a license.

1. Have your business location inspected.
2. Complete an application.
3. Take a dealer orientation class.
4. Purchase a bond in the amount of $15,000.
5. Submit all your paperwork to MVA, BL&CS.

Massachusetts

You need a license to sell vehicles in the state of Massachusetts.

1. Complete the following forms:

a. Zoning Application Form

b. Articles of Organization

c. Purchase and Sale Agreement

d. Lease Agreement

e. Workers Compensation Insurance Affidavit

2. Purchase a bond in the amount of $25,000.

3. Submit everything to your local municipality and pay the fee of $200.

Michigan

You will need a license if you sell over 5 vehicles in a 12 month period.

1. Complete an application packet.
2. Have your fingerprints run.
3. Get a Sales Tax Number.
4. Purchase a bond in the amount of $10,000.
5. Submit everything to the Michigan Department of State.

Licenses are good for one year and expire on December 31st.

Minnesota

If you sell over 5 vehicles a year, you need a license.

1. Complete the application.
2. Make sure your location meets the requirements.
3. Complete a Zoning Approval form.
4. Purchase a bond in the amount of $50,000.
5. Provide a Certification of Compliance with Minnesota Workers Compensation Law.
6. Provide Verification of Property Lease or proof of ownership.
7. Provide proof of signage.
8. Submit everything to Minnesota DPS.

Licenses expire in one year.

Mississippi

Anyone selling vehicles needs to get a license.

1. Complete an application.
2. Provide the following:
   a. $100 application fee

    b. Salesperson application and the associated fee

    c. Biography of each principal/owner

    d. Latest financial statement

    e. Pictures of business location

    f. Marketing analysis

3. Purchase a bond in the amount of $25,000.

4. Submit paperwork to the Mississippi Motor Vehicle Commission.

Missouri

If you sell more than six vehicles a year, you need a license.

1. Establish a place of business.

2. Complete an application.

3. Have your location inspected.

4. Submit a background check.

5. Register your business name.

6. Purchase insurance.

7. Purchase a bond in the amount of $50,000.

8. Attend a dealer educational seminar.

9. Submit everything to the Motor Vehicle Bureau.

Licenses expire on December 31st of each year.

Montana

You will need to get a license to sell vehicles in the state of Montana.

1. Complete an application.
2. Purchase a bond in the amount of $50,000.
3. Have your location inspected.
4. Submit everything to the Title and Registration Bureau along with a fee of $30-$500 depending on your application.

Licenses expire on December 31st of each year and cost $30 to renew.

Nebraska

You need a license to sell vehicles in the state of Nebraska.

1. Complete an application.
2. Purchase a bond in the amount of $50,000.
3. Submit the following additional documents:

a. Proof of liability insurance.

b. Proof of workers compensation insurance.

c. Copy of franchise agreement if applicable.

d. Photographs of the business.

e. Copy of a lease agreement, if applicable.

f. Pass local zoning.

4. Submit paperwork to the Nebraska Motor Vehicle Industry Licensing Board.

5. Pass location inspection.

Licenses are good for one year and expire on December 31st.

Nevada

If you sell vehicles in the state of Nevada, you need a license.

1. Complete an application for a business license.

2. Purchase a bond in the amount of $100,000.

3. Purchase liability insurance.

4. Pay the $126 processing fee.

5. Submit all additional paperwork to the Nevada DMV.

Licenses are good for one year.

New Hampshire

You need a license to sell over 5 vehicles a year.

1. Establish a place of business with the following specifications:
   a. At least 750 square feet for selling vehicles.
   b. A business sign on a public street with 10-inch letters.
   c. A permanent heating system.
2. Complete an application.
3. Submit a $125 application fee.
4. Complete a Service Agreement.
5. Pass a criminal background check.
6. Purchase a bond in the amount of $25,000.
7. Submit all paperwork to the Department of Safety.

8. Pass a location inspection.

Licenses expire on March 31st of each year.

New Jersey

Anyone selling vehicles in New Jersey needs a license.

1. Complete the application packet.
2. Include the following with your packet:
    a. Copy of driver's license for each owner.
    b. Color photograph, passport size of each owner.
    c. Copy of Incorporation/Formation papers.
    d. Copy of property of deed or lease.
    e. Copy of Federal EIN Registration Certificate.
    f. Copy of NJ Certificate of Authority for Sales Tax.
3. Pay the $100 license fee and $257.50 registration fee.
4. Mail the packet and documents to the New Jersey Motor Vehicle Commission.
5. Obtain liability insurance.

6. Purchase a bond in the amount of $10,000.

Licenses expire on March 31st of each year.

New Mexico

To sell vehicles in New Mexico, you need a license.

1. Establish a place of business.
2. Complete the following application forms:
    a. Dealer License
    b. Information Form
    c. Affidavit Form
3. Complete a Pre-License Education Class
4. Purchase a bond in the amount of $50,000.
5. Submit everything to the New Mexico Motor Vehicle Division.

Licenses are good for one year and expire March 31st.

New York

You will need a license to sell more than five vehicles in a year in New York.

1. Complete an application.
2. Purchase a bond for $20,000 if under 50 vehicles sold a year.
3. Pay a $37.50 application fee and a $450 registration fee.
4. Submit documents to the Bureau of Consumer and Facility Services.

Licenses are good for two years.

North Carolina

You will need a license to sell more than five vehicles a year.

1. Complete an application and meet requirements.
2. Pass a dealership inspection.
3. Purchase a bond in the amount of $50,000.
4. Complete a licensing course.
5. Pay any associated fees.
6. Submit everything to the North Carolina Department of Transportation.

North Dakota

Anyone selling vehicles in North Dakota needs to get a license.

1. Establish a place of business that meets requirements.
2. Complete an application.
3. Purchase a bond in the amount of $25,000.
4. Pay any associated fees.
5. Submit everything to the Department of Transportation.

Licenses expire every year on December 31st.

Ohio

You need a license if you sell more than five cars in a period of 12 months.

1. Have a verifiable net worth of $75,000
2. Complete an application
3. Submit pictures of the car lot
4. Pay the fees
    a. $50 permit

     b. $50.25 for dealer plates

     c. $150 for Title Defect Rescission Fund

     d. $4.50 postage

5. Complete and submit proof of a used car dealer training course

6. Submit a background check and fingerprinting for each owner, president, partner, and trustee

7. Your dealership must meet the correct physical characteristics

Licenses expire on March 31 every 2 years.

Oklahoma

A license is required to sell vehicles in the state of Oklahoma.

1. Complete an application.
2. Complete a salesperson license application.
3. Purchase a bond in the amount of $25,000.
4. Pay any associated fees.
5. Submit your application and forms to the Used Motor Vehicle and Parts Commission.

Licenses expire on December 31st in odd-numbered years.

Oregon

In order to sell vehicles in Oregon, you need to get a license.

1. Complete an application.
2. Purchase liability insurance.
3. Purchase a bond in the amount of $50,000.
4. Get an Education Certificate.
5. Pay associated fees.
6. Submit everything to the DMV Business License Unit.

Pennsylvania

You will need a license to sell more than 5 vehicles a year.

1. Establish a place of business according to requirements.
2. Complete an application.
3. Purchase a bond in the amount of $20,000.

4. Submit everything to the Department of Transportation.
5. Pass a location inspection.

Licenses expire on May 31st in odd-numbered years.

Rhode Island

You will need a license to sell over four vehicles a year in Rhode Island.

1. Establish a place of business according to requirements.
2. Get your dealership name approved.
3. Complete an application.
4. Purchase a bond in the amount of $50,000.
5. Submit everything to the Department of Motor Vehicles.

Licenses are good for one year and expire on December 31st, but renewals need to be submitted no later than October 31st.

South Carolina

South Carolina requires a license in order to sell vehicles.

1. Attend a pre-licensing course.
2. Complete an application.
3. Purchase a bond in the amount of $30,000.
4. Provide the following additional documents:
   a. Sales tax number.
   b. Incorporation papers.
   c. Proof of liability insurance.
   d. Affidavit of eligibility for each owner of over 10%.
   e. Criminal history report for each owner of over 10%.
5. Submit everything to the Department of Motor Vehicles.
6. Pay any associated fees.

Licenses are valid for one year.

South Dakota

You'll need a license to sell over five vehicles in a 12 month period.

1. Complete an application.
2. Complete an application for dealer plates.
3. Purchase a bond in the amount of $25,000.
4. Pay the $300 fee.
5. Submit everything to the Department of Revenue and Regulation.
6. Pass a dealership inspection.

Licenses are good for five years and cost $175 to renew.

Tennessee

You will need a license to sell over five vehicles a year.

1. Establish a place of business according to requirements.
2. Have your business inspected.
3. Complete an application.

4. Purchase a bond in the amount of $50,000.

5. Submit an information packet.

6. Pay any associated fees.

7. Submit everything to the local County Clerk.

Texas

If you sell over five vehicles a year in Texas, you will need a license.

1. Obtain a General Distinguishing Number.

2. Complete an application.

3. Purchase a bond in the amount of $25,000.

4. Submit your application to the Texas DMV.

Licenses are good for two years.

Utah

You will need a license if you plan to sell vehicles in Utah.

1. Complete an application.

2. Complete an FBI fingerprint card.

3. Provide photographs of your business and signage.
4. Purchase a bond in the amount of $75,000.
5. Get a Sales Tax Number.
6. Attend a training seminar.
7. Pay any associated fees.
8. Submit everything to the Motor Vehicle Enforcement Division.

Licenses expire on June 30th of each year.

Vermont

You need a license to sell vehicles in Vermont.

1. Complete an application with associated documentation.
2. Purchase a bond in the amount of $35,000.
3. Submit everything to the Department of Motor Vehicles.
4. Pay any associated fees.

Licenses are good for one year.

Virginia

You will need a license to sell vehicles in Virginia. There are 11 types of licenses, so choose carefully.

1. Complete an application.
2. Complete a dealer-operator training course.
3. Purchase a bond in the amount of $50,000.
4. Pay any associated fees.
5. Submit everything to the Motor Vehicle Dealer Board.

Licenses are good for one year.

Washington

You will need a license to sell over four vehicles a year.

1. Obtain a certificate of dealer education.
2. Establish a business location according to specifications.
3. Complete all necessary paperwork.
4. Sign up for e-permitting.
5. Purchase a bond in the amount of $30,000.

6. Pay the $975 license fee.

7. Submit everything to the State of Washington.

Licenses are good for one year.

West Virginia

You will need a license in order to sell vehicles in West Virginia.

1. Have a pre-inspection of your dealership.
2. Complete an application.
3. Purchase a bond in the amount of $25,000.
4. Mail everything to the Office of Dealer Services.

Licenses expire on June 30th of each year.

Wisconsin

You will need a license if you plan to sell over five vehicles a year.

1. Complete the paperwork package.
2. Purchase a bond in the amount of $50,000.
3. Pay any associated fees.

4. Submit everything to the Department of Transportation.

Wyoming

You will need a license in order to sell more than three vehicles a year.

1. Complete an application.
2. Get a Wyoming Sales and Use Tax License.
3. Get a criminal background check.
4. Submit everything to the Department of Transportation.
5. Purchase a bond in the amount of $25,000.
6. Submit proof of your bond.

Licenses are valid for one year.